REDWOODS
and
ROSES

The Gardening Heritage
of California and the Old West

Maureen Gilmer

Taylor Publishing Company
Dallas, Texas

To the survivors,
Thomas Meriweather Gilmer
and
Jane Cooper Hemphill

The West is dead, my friend,
But writers hold the seed.
And what they saw will live and grow,
Again to those who read.

CHARLES M. RUSSELL, 1917

ALSO BY MAUREEN GILMER:

The Complete Guide To Southern California Gardening
The Complete Guide To Northern California Gardening
California Wildfire Landscaping
The Wildfire Survival Guide
Easy Lawn and Garden Care

Copyright © 1995 Maureen Gilmer

Published by Taylor Publishing Company
1550 West Mockingbird Lane
Dallas, Texas 75235

Designed by David Timmons

Library of Congress Cataloging-in-Publication Data
Gilmer, Maureen.
    Redwoods and roses : the gardening heritage of California and the Old
West / Maureen Gilmer.
        p.   cm.
    Includes bibliographical references (p. 200) and index.
    ISBN 0-87833-894-2
    1. Gardening—California. 2. Gardening—California—History. 3. Plants, Ornamental—Heirloom varieties—California. 4. Heirloom varieties (Plants)—California. 5. Native plants for cultivation—California. I. Title
SB453.2.C3G545 1995
635' .09794—dc20   95-24498
                                                                                          CIP

Printed in the United States of America
10 9   8   7   6   5   4   3   2   1
This book is printed on acid-free paper

CONTENTS

INTRODUCTION

hen I was a young girl, home was the dilapidated town of Calabasas, California, a Spanish name commemorating a load of pumpkins that spilled two centuries ago along El Camino Real, "The King's Road." By the time I arrived, it was no more than a cluster of old buildings nestled in the west end of the San Fernando Valley. During the summers, I was rarely separated from my horse, which carried me to this, the only town within riding distance from my family's house. On the hottest days I would tie that speckled gray mare beneath the huge peppertrees that lined the old road in front of the historic Leonis Adobe. There the huge, pendulous canopies released the scents of their aromatic oils and shaded the ground from the blistering Western sun.

This restored adobe house, now a museum, was once a stop along the ancient Spanish trading artery that linked California's mission chain. The house drew me by some mystical lure—as do many houses, which speak to those who listen. I wandered its cool rooms insulated from the heat and cold by thick mud walls. Though the outsides were encased in board siding and the interior plastered over, the kitchen proved the versatility of clay. Its floor was steel gray, earth-packed, and hard as though fired in a kiln. The surface was buffed to a reflective patina as clean as that of polished stone. Docents told tales

ℛaoul Esnard on his horse Blizzard.

of ghosts, most often that of Miguel Leonis himself, walking the upstairs gallery in the evenings of Catholic feast days.

Sometimes when I lingered beneath the peppertrees, their boughs swaying in the hot Santa Ana winds, I could imagine so clearly another time, when California was but an outpost of Spain thriving on the hide and tallow trade. The now-immense prickly pear hedge at the adobe had once enclosed livestock pens, and the remnants of Castilian roses that had struggled in the yard were now tended with care. And I wondered what the great live oaks had seen over the centuries, for their massive size assured me they were indeed there with the Spanish.

Further to the west my grandfather owned a ranch where he raised thoroughbred horses, a piece of property surrounded by treeless, grassy hills dotted with sorrel mares and their foals. My father often told his six children stories of his own childhood and the white mustang pony Blizzard. Old family photos show a much younger man, relaxed in his saddle with long *tapadera* stirrups that are no longer in style among horsemen. As children, we had no doubt that his tale of rustlers hidden in caves of those same hills was true, but not until adulthood did we discover it was actually a figment of his imagination. Yet that tale left in us a yearning for the Old West that remains strong today after nearly four decades.

As a teen I knew the daughter of one of Santa Barbara's oldest families, the de la Guerras. On a visit with her to the ancestral ranch granted the family by the Spanish, I entered the original adobe house. Inside the floors sloped precariously, but the old grace and charm of that era was still plainly felt. The original rooms, with niches in the thick walls and with the high headboards of handcarved California live oak beds, seemed humble compared to improvements added on during Victorian times. But to experience that mystical place and walk where the vaqueros did, to feel in the still air a hint of old land grants, was unforgettable. Even the fine bedrock mortars and metates arranged about the property suggested a dreamy journey back in time, a retreat to the California of yesterday, a rare glimpse of the Old West firsthand.

From these experiences of early life, I have grown attached to things of the West; as a lover of gardens, studying the relationships of plants to these pioneers is the most direct way to evoke early California. In our land of little rain, it makes no sense to seek out gardens of the East, or even those of Europe, where rainfall is more frequent. In the West our natural history contains some of the most lasting images of a young country, growing and forever moving toward the Pacific. It is a blending of the Latin and the Native American, Anglo miners from the states, and even Russians who jumped ship on the north coast. All came seeking riches in a gathering of the tribes, and there found a home which today is still so beautiful it draws newcomers at ever-growing rates.

In the following pages, you will find our history described in terms of plants that provided a wealth of food and materials—even whole industries—for those who lived here. Some plants are among the myriad native species, many endemic only to California. Others came with the settlers, plants of symbolic value, plants for materials, plants that feed, and those that nurture with cooling shade. And finally, with the close of the nineteenth century, the Old West disappeared beneath the industrial revolution and progress, yet the plants lingered and will rise again in the new Western aesthetic.

Let us never forget that this land is a legacy, long isolated and thus unique, with valleys so fertile they created the ultimate environment for agriculture, with harvests unequalled anywhere in the world. As urbanization displaces the fields, it is our duty to cultivate history, remembering that each plant and historic site has a story— and those species that played essential roles are to be remembered. Come with me on a journey through the Old West, and learn as I have that we indeed live amidst the mystique of old California, so that with our heightened awareness it will not be overlooked in the melee of our rapidly changing world.

A BRIEF HISTORY
OF THE
GOLDEN STATE

*T*here is no state that contains greater contrasts of natural environments than California. The dark, primeval redwood forests of the north differ starkly from the dry coastal scrub behind glittering white sands of the southern beaches. The tallest peak in the contiguous states, Mt. Whitney, lies in the rugged Sierra Nevada Mountains, Muir's range of light that stretches like a spine through much of the state. The fertile Sacramento and San Joaquin valleys are the belly of California, encompassing hundreds of square miles of highly productive farmland fed by drainages of the Sierra's western slopes. To the southeast lie our inland deserts, with Death Valley and its searing heat well below sea level. In contrast, the Mohave Desert, despite its incredibly hot summer temperatures, has supported entire cities by springs and underground rivers. California is a patchwork of widely differing climates, each supporting specific communities of native plant life. This natural diversity helped mold the picture of the Old West we know today, having influenced its development in so many ways.

Before the Spanish explorers first arrived, there was no separation between Mexico and southern California, nor were there boundaries with Oregon, Nevada, and Arizona. This land remained undefined and untouched for millions of years except by the prehistoric peoples who migrated across the land bridge of the Bering Strait and filtered down to populate both American continents.

Remains of some of California's very first human residents, discovered in the La Brea Tar Pits of Los Angeles, are estimated to be 15,000 years old.

For thousands of years, tribal separation and isolation accentuated tribe-specific characteristics. By the 1500s, when the Spanish first arrived, the tribes residing in what is now California were well defined. A.L. Kroeber's famous work, *Handbook of the Indians of California*, sets the estimated population of Native Californians before the Spanish at about 130,000. However, scholars today contend the numbers were far higher—as much as 300,000.

The California Native Americans were separated into dozens of tribes, each with a well-defined homeland. A tribal unit typically numbered about 1,000 people and occupied a relatively small tract of land compared to the vast territories of the desert southwest and Great Plains tribes. This was due to the abundance of food, both of plant and animal origin. There was little need to migrate long distances for food, but smaller scale relocation with the seasons was common.

California Indians were for the most part hunting and gathering tribes, depending on the bounty of native plants for much of their food. An exception were the Yumas, who did plant some crops in the rich silt along the flood plain of the Colorado River. California Indians were superb botanists, with intimate knowledge of every native plant as a source of food or other material goods.

The perpetual gathering often required digging for roots and bulbs in the soil. When Anglo explorers first witnessed this activity, they were quick to call all native California peoples "Diggers," an unflattering name still resented by Native Americans today. After the feats of horsemanship exhibited by Great Plains tribes and the elaborate architecture of southwestern Pueblos, the simplicity of Native Californians was perceived as far more primitive and even backward. But in fact their culture was complex, and they were highly skilled in the utilization of plant materials.

During the 1500s, the Spanish, with their strong foothold in the New World, began to venture north from Mexico into California. The pueblos and presidios they founded were supplied by trading ships called Manila galleons, which crossed the Pacific from Spanish colonies in the Philippine Islands. In need of a port of call on the California coast, an anchorage at Monterey Bay was developed for ships to take on provisions after crossing the Pacific Ocean.

It was not until the 1700s that the chain of twenty-one Catholic missions was begun in California by Fra Junipero Serra. The first, San Diego de Alcala, was established in 1769, but not until 1823 was the final mission, San Francisco Solano, built in the Sonoma Valley. In most cases the mission sites were close to Indian villages, which the Spanish called *rancherias*. With these native people available as both converts and laborers, each mission grew into a concentrated center of agriculture.

The Spanish expansion also included pueblos (villages and settlements) and presidios (military outposts or fortresses), which were built and maintained by soldiers. These outposts were designed to protect Spanish holdings from representatives of other nations, such as the Russian fur traders at Fort Ross, with their foothold on the Northern California coast. The British, already well established in Vancouver, also sailed down the West Coast in search of sea otter and seal pelts. With such encroachment, Spain decreed more widespread settlement of Alta California to further secure the land. But Spanish settlers were reluctant to leave the security of Mexico, or even the pueblos of San Diego and Monterey, for remote ranches in unexplored inland territory peopled with less docile tribes than the neophyte converts at the missions.

To encourage settlement, Spain declared in 1784 that the viceroy, governor, and even military commanders could grant large tracts of land to veteran soldiers. One such grant was made to Sergeant Luis Peralta, a member of the Anza expedition of 1776, who joined Father Serra's travels as guard and Indian fighter. Peralta called his grant Rancho San Antonio, a tract so large it encompassed what is now Oakland, Berkeley, and Alameda. Many other retiring soldiers were provided with similar amounts of land that proved to be massive areas, with boundaries defined only by crude, hand-sketched maps. In some cases there was little more than the signed decree to establish ownership. Later on, after California was ceded to the United States, ownership was contested, and most grants were lost due to lack of documentation.

During these early days, cattle and horses were brought to the missions and pueblos both from Mexico and by sea on the galleons. Over time they multiplied into huge herds that ran wild across the California countryside, where unbroken seas of native grasses provided year-round pasture. The great wild herds of long-horned cattle bore no brands, and ranching consisted of simply roping and butchering in order to harvest the hide and render tallow.

These land grant ranchos developed into isolated pockets of activity sustained by cattle ranching, and they supported a thriving trade with American, British, and Mexican trade ships along the coast. Richard Henry Dana's classic book, *Two Years Before the Mast*, first published in 1840, is a fascinating first-person report of coastal California and the hide and tallow industries.

Each land grant rancho was manned with skilled vaqueros (Spanish cowboys), many of whom were California Native Americans, Mexicans, and those of mixed blood. The worldwide demand for leather made these ranchos so wealthy, their owners dressed in Spanish lace and linen. Although they lived in modest adobe homes, the interiors were filled with furnishings and decorations of the Orient brought on Manila galleons. And it was here, during the fiestas and early rodeos, that the mystique of the Old West began. This legacy of the first vaqueros can still be seen today in many skills and traditions of the American cowboy.

The missions, too, had evolved into highly productive villages.

There grapevines, fruit trees, and row crops were cultivated by the Indians, and the padres engineered California's first aqueducts and trench systems of irrigating the dry land. Plants from the Old World imported by the galleons thrived in the mission gardens, where the climate was similar to that of the Iberian Peninsula. Not only were there food plants, but many ornamentals were grown for shading or as symbols of Catholic religious beliefs to be used on feast days as church decorations.

In 1822 Mexico gained its independence from Spain, with boundaries encompassing much of what is now the southwestern United States. No longer would the California missions be sponsored and defended by Spain. The Native Americans who had settled within the mission structure were left without support, and the impending secularization created much unrest. Within a decade, the highly developed, wealthy mission lands were dissolved, and many conflicts arose concerning their distribution. As the missions then fell into ruin, the agricultural networks of California became more limited, with cattle the chief industry.

Over the next twenty years the United States continued to expand westward. Mountain men seeking beaver pelts were forced to move on to new lands in search of their dwindling game, in the process discovering new passes through the forbidding Sierra Nevada Mountains. In their wake came the first pioneers of the 1840s, some successfully reaching Sutter's Fort through these passes, or by a southern route via Santa Fe that skirted the southern tip of the Sierra. Though this route had its difficulties, it avoided the dreadful winters of the Sierra Nevada and its notoriously unpredictable weather patterns.

The hide and tallow trade continued to be an important industry, and along the coast more American ships entered the coves and bays to load cargo. Whaling ships used Monterey and other presidios as supply stations, and Russians competed with the British for harvests of pelts. Many of the first Anglo settlers in California were sailors who jumped ship in these balmy harbors, and married into prominent Mexican families or opened up business enterprises. Still, the geographic isolation of California and its ownership by Mexico ensured that the population remained scattered.

Texas, an independent republic since 1836, became the twenty-eighth state in 1845. Border and settlement disputes there ignited the Mexican War in 1846, but also figuring in the escalation of hostilities was President Polk's frustration due to his rejected attempts to purchase California and surrounding territories from Mexico. Indeed, in June 1846, just one month after the United States' declaration of war, Anglo settlers at Sonoma began the Bear Flag Revolt, declaring California an independent republic. United States forces stepped in to occupy California, while the war raged mostly south of Texas.

The United States Army took Mexico City in December 1847. Two months later in the Treaty of Guadalupe Hidalgo, Mexico ceded its claims to lands north of the Rio Grande, including Texas, California, and land that has become all or part of our plains and southwestern states. The military retained control of California, with difficulty and without a civil government, until it was admitted to the Union as a free state under the Compromise of 1850.

In the midst of these tumultuous times, in January of 1848, Jim Marshall found gold in the American River, just east of what today is Sacramento, California. It was a discovery that ignited new interest in the Far West, resulting in an immigration rush of unbelievable proportions. The few Americans already in California moved into the Sierra Nevada foothills and began mining the placer deposits in the rivers of the western slopes. Within just a few months, word spread through the States, and newcomers from the East set off in droves for the goldfields. Many went overland, a journey of many months through prairie, mountains, and brutal deserts. A greater number elected to sail around Cape Horn to California or shorten the journey by hiking across the Isthmus of Panama to board steamers which plied the West Coast from Acapulco to San Francisco.

Northern California was suddenly inundated with settlers, mostly miners, but the real wealth was amassed by those who supplied goods and services to the goldfields. Prospectors streamed into the Sierra foothills, driving Native American tribes from their ancestral lands. Those that suffered most were the Miwok and other tribes who had the misfortune to call the richest parts of the Mother Lode their home. The remnants of these tribes, individuals who would not relocate or assimilate, found depleted game, persistent disease, and miners with loaded rifles eager to protect their claims from the "savages."

Beginning in 1849, the population of San Francisco exploded from 812 to over 40,000 by the end of 1850. Wealth poured into the city from the goldfields to support new hotels, gambling halls, and restaurants. Towns sprung up overnight along the trading arteries

San Francisco's Victorian charm.

between the goldfields and San Francisco, with Sacramento and Stockton feeding the southern mines, and Marysville the hub of the north. The waters of the Sacramento, American, and Feather rivers became the linking conduits for steamboats that brought latecomers from the coast to the now well-mined and depleted placer deposits.

The development of large-scale hydraulic mining later during the Gold Rush would have a catastrophic impact on the north state. Devastating tailings or "slickens" from eroded mountains of ancient placer deposits were dumped into the rivers. So much material was moved that many rivers were disfigured, wildlife destroyed, and the flow of water diminished. The Middle Fork of the Yuba River today looks like nothing but fine gravel, the unseen water flowing far below the surface. Tailings flowed down into the valley to bury hundreds of acres of the most fertile farmland beneath sterile gravel and sand. Hydraulic mining proved so great an environmental disaster that silt from the Sierra Nevada a hundred miles away was clearly visible in the waters of San Francisco Bay. By the time tailings dumping was outlawed, the riverbeds were already so full that levees were raised still higher and navigation by steamboat was virtually impossible.

With the rising population, statehood soon followed in 1850, and a new economy supported many new industries. Agriculture expanded rapidly to supply the demand for grain and produce in the mining camps as well as the growing cities of the valley and coastal ports. As a newly admitted state, the grab for land inevitably challenged the ownership of early Spanish land grant tracts, and many families of Spanish California struggled to retain their ranchos. But the confusion of a tenuous fledgling government kept verification of title in the courts for years, and legal expenses cost owners their entire fortunes, and ultimately their land as well.

California became a melting pot of Eastern immigrants, as well as Mexicans, Native Americans, and Chinese. The Chinese immigrants also worked the goldfields but were later discouraged by the enactment of a Foreigner Mining Tax. Later many more Chinese were hired by contract from their homeland, then shipped to San Francisco as laborers for construction of the transcontinental railroad. They became an integral part of that city's character and were largely responsible for the arduous task of linking rails across the rugged Sierra Nevada.

During the middle of the nineteenth century, more of California's vast resources were exploited to expand and diversify the economy. Freight and transportation to the mines and outposts of southern California grew into a vast network of roads and rails, with competition among carriers blossoming. Farming expanded to cover more acreage in the Central Valley and spilled into sheltered valleys of various mountain ranges. Wheat, orchards, and row crops were planted, along with new vineyards that revived the wine-making industry, which had been abandoned with the fall of the missions. Cattle ranching continued to remain prominent, with Henry Miller's massive holdings realizing fabulous profits by supplying the mining camps with beef.

The rush of the forty-niners to the goldfields was short-lived, as thousands of prospectors stripped the creeks and rivers of their placer deposits. This yielded to the more costly hardrock quartz gold mines, which were operated by large mining interests based in San Francisco. New silver strikes in Nevada's Comstock Lode drew placer

𝒯his view of Nevada City just after the Gold Rush shows that the surrounding hills are virtually treeless. The forests were logged for miles around to supply shoring timbers for the mines, firewood, and planks for the extensive system of flumes and ditches. Today these hills have regrown their magnificent forests of pine.

miners out of the goldfields to the east slopes of the Sierra; this proved a short yet incredibly rich boom. After the heyday of mining passed, many of the miners remained in California, turning their hands to farming and other new industries. Rivaling the mines in production was the new lumber industry of the northwestern red-wood forests, where the massive trees supplied unlimited amounts of high-quality lumber. The mills built were the largest in the world, in order to accommodate trees of such incredible proportions.

This combination of gold, logging, and agriculture made the middle and latter nineteenth century a time of unbelievable prosperity in California. Revenues supported the expense of a transcontinental railroad over the Sierra Nevada, a feat that finally connected California with the rest of the United States and encouraged a wave of twentieth-century migration.

The climate of newly accessible southern California drew health-seekers and invalids from the cold cities of the East. Not until ambitious water delivery projects were organized and in place did Los Angeles begin to grow and prosper. Agriculture, namely citrus orchards and row crops, also contributed to the latent prosperity of the south. Finally, the discovery and drilling of oil, its refining, and the manufacture of related products brought yet more industry to the area.

The dawning of the twentieth century in California saw growth in all parts of the state. Temperate climate, steady employment, verdant agriculture, and the abundance of land for development created a mecca for new residents. Developers and speculators designed housing tracts and planned communities on a grand scale. Out of the once-prolific beanfields of Los Angeles County rose the palm-lined streets of Beverly Hills.

The heavily ornamented homes of the Victorian era yielded to more conservative dwellings loosely termed bungalows. This was a period when the arts and crafts movement paid tribute to the simplicity of California's earlier days, coupled with a heightened sensitivity to nature. The result was the great achievements of architects Green and Green, who created the consummate bungalow, with every detail carefully designed. To accompany these homes, mission-style furniture replaced baroque Victorian pieces, and today this timeless style is again popular. Perhaps this is in step with our greater awareness of nature and the environment.

The gardens of the bungalow concentrated not on botanical diversity, but on a more basic scheme which would not overwhelm the subtleties of the architecture. The private home garden finally became the domain of everyone, not just the more economically successful class. Nowhere but in California did these gardens take on such a style of their own, and for the first time the great diversity of species allowed by our climate was put to better uses than carpet bedding or conservatories.

The early 1900s held the seeds of today's gardens. The most profound difference from its Victorian predecessor is that the bungalow garden married the outdoors to the indoors much the same way as the Spanish did with their courtyards, verandas, and *huertas*. Mild climate allowed outdoor living year-round in the Southland and most of the time in the north. The notion of extending interior square footage through large doorways and grand patios allowed smaller homes a taste of Victorian grandeur.

There is no one who influenced this movement more than landscape architect Thomas D. Church. He cast off the constraints dictating that a garden was for viewing, not living. His new approach was that smaller homes, tighter lots, and the nuclear family without domestic servants called for a landscape better tailored to modern lifestyles. Where the Victorians placed great emphasis on frontyards to express economic or social success, the bungalow turned its face to the rear, where the family spent most of its time.

With function as the new goal of a landscape, the designs were streamlined, were simple to maintain, and utilized a more organized planting scheme. The Church gardens still drew from the best ideas produced over centuries in European and Arab landscapes, but the new design concepts used line and spatial layout to create forms corresponding with the functions of everyday life.

The future of California gardens will be governed by one crucial factor: water. Our population is growing faster than the existing water delivery system can manage, and when supplies run low, as they did during the last drought, water rationing is inevitable. It is likely rationing will occur again, perhaps permanently—and not necessarily because of drought, but due to the increased demands of a burgeoning population. Therefore, it is a certainty that the picture of California landscapes is destined to change again, this time to a dryland approach.

It is always interesting to look back at history and be reminded that it indeed repeats itself in so many ways. The native plants essential to the California Indians are suddenly made priceless by their perfect adaptation to limited rainfall. This places the work of Lester Rowntree and her precious flowering shrubs of California in the forefront of our garden literature. Plants grown on ranchos and missions, such as the olive tree, are also natural candidates for future California. Those introduced species from dry Africa, Mexico, and Australia popularized and propagated by Kate Sessions suddenly become the saviors of our threatened landscapes.

In the larger scheme of things, it is the plants of California's illustrious past that promise a living future. The Old West was indeed

an era when only the strong survived, be they people, animals, or plants. The world need not discover new species, for the right plants have been here under our noses all the time. Only now, when we have no other choice but to go "dry," does the value of the old ones seem so much greater in our estimation. Perhaps they are assured another chance to become the stars of the California landscape once again.

RED EARTH AND ACORNS

The white people never cared for land or deer or bear.
When we Indians kill meat we eat it all up. When we dig
roots we make little holes. When we build houses we make
little holes. When we burn grass for grasshoppers we don't
ruin things. We shake down acorns and pine nuts. We don't
chop down the trees. We use only dead wood. But the white
people plow up the ground, pull up the trees, kill everything.
OLD WINTU WOMAN, 1930

*I*t is estimated that the California Native American tribes and subtribes just prior to the mission era numbered at least one hundred. Their great diversity of languages stemmed from a variety of basic groups of people who gradually migrated from the north and east to settle in the verdant landscape of California. Only the Yukian tribes, which lived in northern Mendocino County, are unique, their language having no similarity to that of any other American tribe. These, some say, are the only true Native Californians.

The California tribes were very peaceful people and obtained their provisions through a great knowledge of local plants and their uses. The ethnologist Robert Heizer divides the California tribes into

TRIBES OF EACH CULTURAL AREA
DEPICTED ON MAP

Northwest Tolowa, Karok, Shasta, Yurok, Whilkut, Hupa, Chimariko

Northeast Modok, Achomawi, Atsugewi

Central Mattole, Nongati, Wintu, Yana, Yahi, Lassik, Sinkyone, Wailaki, Kato, Yuki, Maidu, Pomo, Lake Miwok, Interior Miwok, Wappo, Coast Miwok, Coastanoan, Esselen, Yokuts, Monache, Salinan

Great Basin Northern Paiute, Washoe, Mono Paiute, Owens Valley Paiute, Panamint Shoshoni, Tubatulabal, Kawaiisu, Vanyume, Chemehuevi

Southern Chumash, Akiklik, Kitanemuk, Fernandeno, Gabrielino, Serrano, Luiseno, Juaneno, Cupeno, Cahuilla, Diegueno, Kamia

Colorado
River Mohave, Halchidhoma, Yuma

six basic groups, primarily based on their local ecology, which influenced what plants were used in their material culture. One native group inhabited the extreme northwest corner of the state, and another the northeast. The third and largest was the Central group, which extended the entire length of the Sacramento and San Joaquin valleys, and westward from the Sierra to the coast. The Great Basin group lined the border with Nevada and Arizona, covering the east slopes of the Sierra and much of the inland desert. The Southern group extended from around Santa Barbara southward to the Mexican border and inland to the eastern Mohave. And finally the Colorado River group lived in the extreme southeastern corner of the state along the river plains.

The role of native plants varied in each of these cultural groups. In terms of food, the valley and plains gatherers lived primarily on a staple of acorns, while the diet of coastal sea hunters consisted mostly of fish. Material cultures also varied between the groups, and a good example is the differing methods of boat building. The north coast peoples hollowed out redwood tree trunks for deep, ocean-going craft. Tule bundled into canoelike rafts were used on shallow inland waterways and bays. In southern California, where these materials were scarce, unique boats of flat planks sewn together and caulked with asphaltum or *brea* proved successful.

Recent studies of northern California tribes have proved Native Californians propagated desired vegetation. This is most apparent in the practices of women gathering basket making materials, as well as some food plants. The women knew that the demand for materials could quickly exhaust the supply, so various techniques of dividing and replanting became widely practiced.

The Native Californians saw that regular harvesting of willow and redbud, for example, could exhaust the plants, which failed to regenerate fast enough to supply the material needs of the tribe. Certain types of growth, such as long, thin whips of fresh sprouts, were most valuable to basket makers. It is now becoming clear that the tribes burned a redbud by creating a mound of fuel over the plant and setting it aflame. This burned off all the stiff, knotted old growth so that the following year only long, thin, whiplike growth sprouted from the root crown. Redbud, like many other shrubs of the chaparral, evolved to survive fire by quickly resprouting from the root crowns. When fire suppression discouraged this practice, the women began hand-pruning wild plants to encourage new growth of the sort of material they preferred. Likewise, in order not to exhaust the availability of roots and bulbs, they replanted a certain portion of them. Plants were encouraged to grow in new locations, as well, to create a greater abundance of gathering opportunities.

Of all the California tribes, those which occupied the Sacramento and San Joaquin valleys were the wealthiest, as food was most abundant there. The routes of migrating waterfowl follow the length of this valley, which before settlement was a massive wetland. The tribes which lived here not only had acorn for a staple food, but hunting was simple, using a variety of methods from snares to arrows. As with all cultures, the abundance of food promoted more leisure time, during which the people developed elaborate material arts and religions.

California tribes did not often migrate long distances. But to harvest certain crops and when local supplies were limited by flood or drought, then the people were forced to seek out more distant and unusual food sources. Foothill tribes annually moved up into the Sierra and other mountain ranges for the summer to hunt and gather. They followed deer herds, which also sought out the succulent grasses of higher meadows when the lower hills were brown and dry. Often different tribes would meet at mountain camps and trade their resources, such as soaproot and pigments. The Washoe and other desert tribes migrated at the time of piñon nut harvest to higher country, where the groves were located.

Throughout the Sacramento Valley, Native Californians built up large mounds of soil from fifty to one hundred feet across along the rivers. These consisted of silt which raises the living areas above the wetlands and seasonal flooding. During the summer, valley people faced intense summer heat, tule fires, and incredible insect hordes breeding in the marshy ground. It is believed that many abandoned their mounds and moved to the surrounding hills for a few months out of the year. Although most of these mounds were leveled by farmers earlier in this century, some remain today because they were conveniently incorporated into the levee systems.

Fire played an important part in the land management practiced by many tribes throughout the state. In order to clear chaparral and forest land for hunting, they regularly burned it. This not only facilitated movement in these areas, but it also increased visual distance in order to see game. But burning was proved by foresters to increase the density of game as well. In a recent test, foresters determined the deer population in a certain foothill area was about 30 animals per square mile. The first year after a controlled burn, the density rose to 98 per square mile. The second year there were 131 per square mile. This was attributed to the fact that fire-burned ground tended to sprout more feed, which actually would increase the number of animals available to Indian hunters. After the Gold Rush, burning was no longer practiced, and fire was suppressed whenever possible. As a result, the overgrowth and deep layers of forest litter now fuel such hot and long-burning fires that they cause total devastation.

Some tribal groups developed very strong dependence on particular plants. Perhaps the most well known is the oak tree acorn, a staple food throughout most of the state. But the most interesting dependence was exhibited by the Cahuilla, a desert tribe which once occupied the palm groves of Agua Caliente, which is today the Palm Springs area. These people lived primarily an isolated existence and developed a productive relationship with our only native palm species. Many of the north coast tribes relied heavily on the California redwood trees, which provided an easily worked wood for both dwellings and boats. Its resistance to decomposition was of primary importance; outside this region similar relationships occurred with native cedar.

The peacefulness of the California tribes played a part in their ultimate demise. A naturally trusting nature made them vulnerable to the Spanish missionaries because they could be organized and put to work with very little resistance. As a result, the Indians left their traditional ways and became dependent on the mission system. With secularization the neophytes suddenly found themselves without support and less able to return successfully to their old ways. Inland tribes untouched by the missions retained their traditional ways, although they too had some contact with such early landowners as John Sutter.

Disease was one of the greatest enemies of the Native Californian tribes, for centuries of isolation had left them with little immunity to even simple illnesses such as colds and flu. Introduction of more virulent organisms, like syphilis and smallpox, caused devastating epidemics. Wherever there was contact with European and American settlers, the diseases followed and people died.

The final blow was the massive rise in immigrant populations during the Gold Rush, and it was then that the insulting name of "Digger" was given to these native botanists. Their perpetual digging for the roots of the soap plant and the cattail, along with stooped gathering of acorns, was perceived by the whites as rooting in the earth, and the unflattering term was applied to all California Native Americans. During the Mexican period, many neophytes left homeless by the mission changes turned to the ranches, where they worked for food and a place to sleep. This increased their familiarity with horses and cattle. Raiding by "wild" Indians degraded all Native Americans even further in the eyes of white settlers.

By the time of the Gold Rush, it was not uncommon for Indians to be shot simply for amusement. What were once tribal hunting lands became prime placer mining areas, where the creeks and rivers were literally exploded to obtain alluvial gold from deep gravel deposits. With the incredibly destructive hydraulic mining, large- scale riparian devastation occurred throughout the west slopes of the Sierra and down through the valley drainages. During the late nineteenth century, California Indians were driven onto *rancherias* or concentrated villages such as Round Valley, where the remaining population lived until official reservations were established by the United States government. Today many of the tribes have died out entirely, and others struggle to retain their vanishing identities.

The humble and quiet life of our local Native Americans has been overshadowed by the glorious legends of the warlike tribes of the Great Plains. Yet, here the people lived off the wealthy ecosystems in harmony with each other and their surroundings for centuries. Their decline was rapid after the mission era, and by the time the Americans reached California in significant numbers, the population of Native Californians was already greatly reduced through disease and assimilation into the less racially divided Mexican culture.

Today we may still appreciate the same native plants that were essential to these early tribes. Some Native Americans, such as Julia Parker, a Yosemite Miwok, strive to retain the old ways so they may be appreciated by the coming generations. Only through dedicated souls like Julia will we ever understand how fully these first residents depended on wild plants for survival, for the story of our native plants cannot be told without presenting the role they played in the heritage and cultures of these skilled Native Peoples.

THE FLORA OF THE NATIVE AMERICANS

Oaks and Acorns
Quercus spp.

One of the finest books ever written on the art of acorn preparation, *It Will Live Forever*, written by Beverly Ortiz, profiles Julia Parker and her lifelong study of the old methods as taught by her aunt, Lucy Telles. Ortiz has brought the subtleties of this ancient food source to light in exquisite detail. The book also details the harvest of soaproot, extraction of the soapy pulp, and the preparation of soaproot brushes. The book includes details on basket design and grinding methods, and most importantly clarifies numerous misunderstandings regarding the entire process of making acorn.

Tourists in California most often comment that the rolling, grassy hills and oak trees are the most picturesque features of our landscapes. There are about fifteen different species of oaks native to California, distributed throughout the entire state in various plant communities. For the untrained eye, the subtle distinctions between oak species are difficult to see, the main differences being overall size and whether the species is evergreen or deciduous. Only about seven of these fifteen species were widely used by Native Californians.

Oak trees reproduce heavily by acorns, which are nuts with nutritious meat inside a hard shell. California tribes living off acorns fared better nutritionally than others outside the oak-bearing areas. For example, the black oak (*Quercus Kelloggii*) acorn contains about 3.5% protein, 13.5% fat, and 42% carbohydrates. Only the Washoe had access to similar nutrition, although their piñon nuts were far smaller and took more time to extract the meat. In addition, the piñon nuts did not keep well, often failing to last the winter.

The acorn crop is not consistent, varying from year to year, depending on the species. The valley oak (*Quercus lobata*) produces a heavy crop every third year or so, and very few acorns mature during the interim years. For this reason tribes sometimes traveled short distances to harvest crops from alternate species. Most tribes constructed elevated acorn granaries of twigs and brush, where they could store up to two years' supply. Boughs of fresh cedar foliage or those of the pungent California bay (*Umbellularia californi-ca*) were used to discourage insect damage to acorns inside granaries. To discourage rodents and other climbing vermin, the poles supporting the granaries were smeared with pitch. If this were still not enough, there were many other food sources, from dried fish to buckeye, which were sufficient to prevent any serious famine.

One interesting relationship occurs between woodpeckers and the black oak (*Quercus Kelloggii*), which is easily identified by its large leaves and habita-tion of more mountainous inland regions. The wood-pecker feeds on many types of acorns, but in lean years it will store them for winter use. The bird drills a large hole in the bark of the black oak and inserts an acorn from any other oak tree, with the pointed end first. He hammers it in tightly until flush with the outside of the tree to prevent squirrels from stealing it. Some trees, as well as fence posts and power line poles, are peppered with acorns, which may remain in place for many years. The Native Californians understood this and, during lean times, often went in search of these "woodpecker oaks" and extracted the nuts for themselves.

Black Oak
(*Quercus Kelloggii*)

The California tribes are the finest basket makers in North America, and the acorn preparation process relied heavily on a series of specially designed baskets. These included conical burden or gath-ering baskets, openly woven sifters, flat winnowing trays, and the famous, watertight cooking baskets. Preparing acorn was strictly the task of women, who took great pride in performing each step as per-fectly as possible.

In their gathering lands, trees were often the property of indi-viduals or families, and gatherers took care to never break a branch or damage the trees. They always left some acorns behind to feed wildlife and generate new trees. In the Sierra foothills acorns were gathered when the leaves on the black oaks turned yellow in the fall. And gath-ering, as Julia Parker tells us, was not simply collecting, but the care-ful selection of only perfect acorns, a far more time-consuming task than simply scooping quantities into baskets.

Acorns could be prepared fresh or dried whole and stored inside the granaries. There is evidence that a few tribes buried their acorns whole in wet, marshy ground and let them remain for a year. The

Sheltered beneath a brush arbor covered with blankets and cloth, this woman's baskets illustrate the types used in making acorn flour. On the left is the large, conical gathering basket, which would be strapped to her back. To the right of the woman is a flat winnowing tray, which contains fresh acorns still in their shells. On the far right is a special basket for sifting newly crushed acorn meats to separate out any larger chunks, which would be returned to the bedrock mortar for further pulverization. (*Stellman Collection, California State Library*)

result was purple-colored acorns whose tannin had been reduced to such an extent that they could be immediately consumed. Another method stored shelled acorns in baskets until they developed mold. Then the basket and its contents were buried in riverbed sand until they turned black, with no further tannin leaching needed.

But these methods were the exception, with most tribes following similar preparation methods of their acorn crops. The first step was to crack the shells with specially selected stones, then extract the meats. These are like a peanut, shrouded in a paper-thin layer, which was winnowed off. Then the soft meats were crushed into a meal. This was done in either portable grinding bowls or in the deep bedrock mortars still evident today in granite boulders throughout much of

Valley Oak
(*Quercus lobata*)

the state. Acorn nuts naturally contain bitter tannic acid, which was leached with fresh water run through the acorn meal. This was done on the sandy banks of a waterway, where a hole was dug, lined with leaves, and the meal placed inside. Water was gently poured through fir boughs until tasting proved the leaching process was complete.

Acorn flour or meal was cooked into porridge, cakes, or a gruel fed to small children. The method of cooking within tightly coiled cooking baskets was unique to western tribes. The basket was filled with acorn meal and water. Carefully chosen smooth stones about the size of baseballs were preheated in the fire. One stone would be retrieved with wooden tongs, then dipped in fresh water to remove the ash, before setting it gently into the watery meal. After a short time it was removed and replaced by another heated stone. This process continued until the water was heated to boiling, and it took a practiced hand to know exactly when to remove the rocks, as they could easily burn through the bottom of the basket.

The valley oak was the species of greatest value to tribes in the California lowlands, where it grows to incredible proportions, with gracefully pendulous branches and deeply furrowed bark. Named for its preference for inland valley soils, this deciduous oak draws off abundant groundwater, which protects it from drought. Originally valley oaks were spread out from Los Angeles to the northern reaches of the Sacramento Valley, where groves studded the grassy plain, making it look like an enormous landscaped park.

A large specimen could produce an acorn crop weighing in excess of a thousand pounds, and the extensive groves ensured local tribes of an abundance of food. It is estimated that only a tiny portion of the annual acorn crop was utilized by native peoples. The harvest of the valley oak lasted about two weeks each year, with entire families pitching in together to gather the nuts while they were fresh and unblemished.

In 1796 Captain George Vancouver saw the trees in the Santa Clara Valley and thought them nearly identical to the mighty oaks of England, which were a precious but dwindling resource to shipbuilders of that day. Despite the visual similarity, the wood of the valley oak is not suitable for building, being of twisted grain, extremely heavy, and brittle. Early attempts by the Spanish to repair their ships with its wood proved disastrous.

The valley oak has also been called the Forty-niner's Tree for it grew quite large in the gold country. In the mining camp of Big Oak Flat was an enormous specimen with a trunk measuring eleven feet in diameter. It became a landmark, and the miners passed a law to preserve it. However, as the men tore up the earth to extract their precious metal, the roots and soil of this beloved tree were damaged, and it was soon lost to erosion.

The famous oak Hangman's Tree in Tuolumne County, a beautiful example of the large, old trees found by the forty-niners in the southern Mother Lode. (*California State Library*)

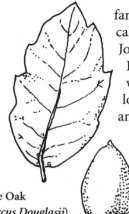

Blue Oak
(*Quercus Douglasii*)

In the town of Chico, founded by the famous General Bidwell, grew a massive tree called the Hooker Oak, for it was visited by Sir Joseph Hooker, director of Kew Gardens, England, who deemed it the largest oak in the world. Unfortunately, the majority of these lovely old trees have been lost to agriculture and development because they thrived on the most fertile farmland; the subsequent leveling and cultivation were their downfall.

The coast live oak (*Quercus agrifolia*) is the only native species that is widely used for landscaping purposes. Not only does it have a unique, gnarled shape, it is more forgiving of container culture. It grows naturally over a very large area along the California coast, stretching from the Mexican border to above the San Francisco Bay. Just as the valley oak will not grow close to the coastline, the coast live oak will not grow successfully very far inland. The tribes of southern and coastal central California relied heavily on the acorns of the live oak.

The Spanish first named the evergreen coast live oak *encina* after a similar evergreen species of oak in the Mediterranean region. One large specimen marked the sites of Fra Junipero Serra's first landing in California and his initial Indian conversion to Christianity. These naturally twisted oaks once covered an astounding amount of land in coastal communities. Its wood was more reliable for shipbuilders, and many old trees were cut down for repairs by explorers, with the crotches particularly valued for curved segments.

But it was the need for heating fuel that spelled the demise of our once extensive coast live oak woodlands. Ships trading along the coastline put in to shore frequently to replenish their supply of cooking fuel. The cord wood of live oak burned not only longer

Live Oak
(*Quercus agrifolia*)

but hotter as well; on board ships, where space was limited, the increased efficiency of this fuel was a premium. Groves were decimated well before the American era, although destruction increased with the demands of a rising population after the Gold Rush.

California Fan Palm
Washingtonia filifera

Step out of the lush resorts of Palm Springs, and you are assaulted by an incredibly barren landscape of rock and sand, with summer temperatures that easily exceed 120 degrees F. Yet hidden away in these rugged hills are isolated springs, shaded by groves of California's only native palm. Climb down the trail at Agua Caliente into Palm Canyon, and the change from harsh desert to a dark and cool grove is startling. It seems truly a miracle to find an inviting haven amidst such brutal desert. For eons the Cahuilla Indians have lived beneath the protective shade of this and a few smaller groves, thriving on a unique ecosystem sustained by groundwater springs. Still more of these isolated groves are scattered throughout our southern deserts and down into Baja California.

The California fan palm, also known as the desert fan palm, appears very similar to its close relative, the much taller and faster growing Mexican fan palm (*Washingtonia robusta*). The most distinctive feature of our palms is the grass skirt of dry fronds that remain attached by their stems to the trunk after they wither. A palm may have its entire trunk shrouded in these fronds, and the fact they remain in place for decades attests to the fibers' resistance to decomposition. Only high winds and flash flooding can naturally dislodge them.

The native people of these desert communities efficiently used virtually every part of the palms in their material culture. Fronds made a plentiful and long-lasting thatch for huts, and similar palm roofs are still used today in Baja California over adobe homes. The Cahuilla also wove the fibrous blades into fine baskets, rope, and sandals. Native people used tender new shoots to make their own version of the large sombrero long before the Spanish arrived, and for the infrequent rains they also used a cape of palm leaves. A version of this cape as well as palm-fiber sombreros were well-known hallmarks of Mexican vaqueros of Yaqui ancestry.

The long petioles, or leaf stalks, of the fronds are stiff and quite woody, the edges lined with a row of sharp thorns. But with trees scarce in the desert, these and the rigid fruiting stems (spadices) provided wood for essential everyday implements used in hunting, building, and cooking.

In the late summer and fall, the palms also provided food on the ends of long spadices, which originate deep inside the foliage head. I have seen tall specimens of these palms in the Sacramento Valley produce enormous bloom spadices, which may extend a dozen feet beyond the fronds in a series of graceful arching bowers, which are unfortunately far too high up for the less palm-minded of us to appreciate. But the Cahuilla depended on them for food, and each tree averaged about seven spadices per palm, with each spadix producing up to forty pounds of fruit. During wet years the Indians harvested somewhere in the neighborhood of three hundred pounds per tree.

The fruit is small, with a hard, black shell that discourages insects from reaching the flesh and seed inside. The Indians ate them fresh, but they also dried and stored them for the winter in ceramic jars. The dried flesh was so hard it required soaking before being ground up much the same way as acorns on a bedrock mortar. The resulting meal was eaten cooked as a mush. During droughts the hearts of the palms were also eaten, but only as a famine food, for it killed the trees to lose the soft, growing tissue inside the foliage head. Like the Washoe, who protected their piñon groves, and the Miwok, with their reverence for the oak, there is no doubt the Cahuilla found it equally difficult to injure or kill their palms even under the most trying circumstances, knowing it would reduce their harvests of fruit in the future.

The Cahuilla used fire as a management tool, burning the accumulations of thatch from their palms on a regular basis. Burning was done during wet weather in winter, because in drier months the flames could ignite serious fires that would kill the palms. Palms were burned for a variety of reasons. First, burning cleaned the trunks and made them easier to climb when harvesting the fruit stalks. Burning also eliminated the danger of the heavy, thorn-studded fronds from falling upon dwellings or residents.

But the Cahuilla themselves said it was done "to get rid of the bugs," the bugs being the giant palm boring beetle and its destructive tunneling larvae. The beetles enter the palm through the soft, newly forming growing tip of the foliage, where they lay their eggs. Later voracious larvae tunnel through the center of the palm and can easily kill the trees.

But just as burning chaparral increased the deer populations in the Sierra foothills, it has been proven that burning palms encourages more prolific fruiting. A study of over three hundred of these palms proved trees burned within the previous four years produced about sixty percent more fruit, thus attesting to the value of the Native American fire management technique.

A fourth reason for burning is to reduce competition by riparian trees such as cottonwoods and willows, which also inhabit the palm oases. These weedy saplings were burned out, thus reducing the overall demand of vegetation for limited groundwater, ensuring more was available for the palms.

From these groves came thousands of palm seedlings which are now planted in gardens and cities the entire length of the state. They make fine landscape trees: A mature linear planting at the Sacramento Capitol building illustrates their uniformity of growth and overall beauty. During the freeze of 1990, the California fan palms fared much better than the Mexican fan palms, proving the natives are far more tolerant of varying conditions farther north. They can also be more expensive to buy because nurseries must contend with their growth rate being slower than the Mexican cousins'. Beware when buying fan palms because when young, there is very little difference between the Mexican and far more valuable California fan palms.

Digger Pine
Pinus sabiniana

Throughout the Coast Ranges and in the lower Sierra Nevada foothills, wispy heads of digger pines rise far above the surrounding oak woodlands. They are more prevalent on the poorest of ground, with some of the best examples on steep, rocky walls which drop precariously down to the many rivers of the western Sierra drainages. The nearly vertical cliffs are sometimes well forested with the massive trunks and blue-gray clouds of digger foliage leaning precariously out over the chasms. This illustrates the tenacity of this tree, which was an essential source of food and materials for many Native Californian tribes.

Native Americans do not judge a tree for its landscape value. A species as generous as the digger pine can be valued almost as a spiritual entity. During years of poor acorn harvest, foothill tribes relied more heavily on digger pine for its large, nutritious nuts. Lodged inside tight, cruelly spiked cones, the nuts could be difficult to extract. They resemble the nuts of the piñon pine of the desert southwest, with a hard outer coating and a soft meat inside similar in size and shape to a kidney bean. To local tribes the nuts not only provided an alternative food source to the acorn, but the meats could be eaten immediately, as they did not contain tannin. The nut shells were also used for beads by grinding off each end of an intact nut and cleaning out the meat, yielding a cylindrical tube which was threaded onto braided bear grass for decorative fronts of women's kilt skirts.

Harvesting of cones began in the spring while they were still green, and if near to the ground, they were beaten off the limbs with sticks. But since diggers tend to produce more cones on the ends of the higher branches, the men sometimes climbed the trees to twist them off by hand. These softer green cones were pounded with a stone until they split apart. The scales are workable at this stage and more easily yield the immature nuts than after the cone has hardened off and become woody. The extracted nuts were pounded into meal or roasted whole. The green core of the cone that resulted after its scales were removed was roasted in hot ashes for twenty minutes or so to yield a pithy but sweet, syrupy food. In September the mature cones that had fallen from the trees were also gathered and dropped whole into a fire to burn off the heavy concentrations of pitch. Then the cone was destroyed to release the nuts, which were cracked for the meats and roasted.

Many of the California tribes lived in conical huts shaped much like tepees, but rigid and constructed by overlaying large slabs of bark or split cedar until the whole was three to four courses thick. They required no additional support and functioned quite well even in the very wet north coast. In the Upper Sonoran zone the favored bark was from the digger pine, which could be easily pried away from the trunks of trees already down and dead.

Digger pines are still maligned today as their gray needles are too frugally dispersed upon the branches to provide any shade at all. They are often thinned out of the landscape because they tend to list precariously even on flat ground. On slopes they also lean outward,

*I*n this Mono settlement, the dwelling is constructed of split cedar boards with a layer of digger pine bark on top. Thatched huts were not suitable for northern tribes, where heavy snowfall required a more rigid material than thatch. In the background is an elevated pine nut granary, and vegetation on surrounding hills includes digger pine and ponderosa pine. (*California State Library*)

rather than standing upright and plumb as other trees do. Digger pines also bear massive, very heavy cones that fall with enough force to seriously wound a person or livestock, not to mention what they'd do to an automobile. As if that were not enough, loggers consider the wood worthless, for it rots and checks terribly after milling. One old-timer was quoted as saying, "Boards from the mill stacked outside to season will walk off overnight." And locals burn digger pine wood for heat only when there is no other fuel to be had, because the pitch can result in chimney fires. Maligned by whites, revered by Native Americans, the digger pine is one of the least understood trees of the West.

Staples of the Desert: Sagebrush, Mesquite, and Piñon

Old cowboy songs of the arid West invariably mention sage or sagebrush. *Artemisia tridentata* is the true sagebrush, a woody shrub bearing the distinctive aromatic foliage and unruly growth habit. This is related to, but not the same as, the garden sages we see today that are organized under the genus *Salvia*. There are also other species of artemisias native to California.

True sagebrush is not a beautiful plant, but its scent provokes visions of a bygone era when cowboys and their mustangs dashed about the badlands after Mexican cows. For me it will always inspire dreams, not of gardens or flowers, but of a wild sense of freedom that is central to the consciousness of every native Westerner.

The Indians widely used sagebrush and its close relatives in association with death. Mourners placed crushed leaves in their nostrils, and rubbed the same upon the corpse to ward off ghosts. Sage was also bundled and strung onto a mourning necklace to discourage dreaming of the dead. For centuries sage and other pungently scented herbs have been used by cultures worldwide in association with funerals. We must remember that under primitive conditions there is no way to control decay of the corpse, which occurs much more quickly in hot weather. It makes sense that the origins of associating sage with death relates to mitigating this problem. It should be noted that in medieval Europe, when bathing was not popular, garden sage and similar herbs were cut and placed in the bedsheets as well as in other strategic places to mask odiferous individuals.

The scented foliage of sagebrush also helped in controlling insects and probably joined other aromatic plants as bedding or floor coverings inside Indian dwellings. Although not often recognized now, fleas and ticks were a common complaint during the early days, and there is no doubt that Californians of any heritage would do whatever possible to prevent their beds from infestation. In fact, the mountain men clung to their buckskin clothing even after cloth was available because the bugs could not lay their eggs or attach themselves as easily to leather.

All California Native American tribes relied on one or all of three staple food sources: mesquite pods, acorns, and piñon nuts. Each was gathered at a certain time and stored for future use. In the desert it was the nutritious pod of the leguminous mesquite tree. In the more arid mountain ranges at about 5,000 feet grew the piñon pines, which bore nuts within their cones.

Mesquite (*Prosopis juliflora*) is a wispy tree that grows in the dry washes of California's southeastern deserts. It is abundantly fruitful and the essential food crop for tribes there. The sweet, syrupy pods contain about 25% sugar. They were gathered, then arranged in the sun to dry before storage. Both the pod and the beans inside were eaten together, usually after being pounded into a nutritious meal. Prior to traveling, the meal was allowed to become sticky, then rolled into dense, compact balls for convenient meals.

The California Native Americans were far more active in managing their wild plants than was originally thought. They increased plant productivity by burning and pruning to encourage certain types of growth. For example, the Cahuilla broke off less productive branches of mesquite trees

A wispy mesquite tree beside the saguaro cactus, one of the West's most easily recognized plants of the desert. Mesquite was a mainstay of many Southern and Colorado River tribes. (*California State Library*)

in order to promote new growth that bore more beans. This was also done to shape the trees so that their branches were closer to the ground and easier to harvest. The Cahuilla regularly set fire to mesquite groves in order to control parasitic mistletoe and encourage more vigorous new growth. Burning also thinned the stands in order to reduce competition among individual trees for what little moisture and nutrients were available in the infertile desert soil.

There is yet more evidence that the Cahuilla dug ditches to

These granaries were made by the Cahuilla people for storage of mesquite pods. As with most Native American granaries, they are elevated upon stout legs, which were sometimes smeared with pitch to prevent pests from climbing into the stored food. These three are expertly woven out of sagebrush twigs, whose aromatic oils will discourage insect pests. (*California Historical Society, Title Insurance and Trust Photo Collection, Department of Special Collections, University of Southern California Library*)

bring water to some of the groves, a rare case of active irrigation by Native Californians. The wood of the mesquite trees is unusually dense and hard, much like that of manzanitas, which were put to similar uses. So durable was mesquite, in fact, that suitable pieces were carved into portable mortars, war clubs, throwing clubs, digging sticks, spears, bows, and arrow shafts. Points were carved at the ends and hardened in fire to become more durable implements and weapons. The branches made the strong structural beams and posts of huts. Even the bark yielded fibers used in basket making.

This wood was preferred for long-lasting and very hot fires used to fire clay pottery, and the charcoal was used for blue-colored tattoos. The charcoal also imparted some flavor to food and is still sought out today in commercially prepared mesquite barbecue briquettes. When wounded, the mesquite tree exudes a gum that was used for glue or boiled down into a black paint for pottery. The boiled gum was also mixed with mud and plastered on the hair, left there a day or two, then washed off. Not only did it leave the hair gleaming, it dyed gray hair black and eliminated head lice as well. Furthermore, the leaves act as a medicinal.

Because these were seasonal harvests, Native Americans were forced to build granaries for storage. The desert tribes chose to weave the young, green branches of sagebrush into a wide but shallow granary about three feet off the ground and supported by stout wood poles. The sage no doubt discouraged any destructive pests or insects from gnawing their way into the stored pods. Likewise, the northern tribes added leaves of fresh cedar (*Librocedrus decurrens*) and California bay (*Umbellularia californica*) to their taller, cylindrical acorn granaries for the same purpose. California bay is closely related to culinary sweet bay (*Laurus nobilis*) and makes a good substitute, with nearly twice the seasoning ability of its anemic European cousin.

The foothill tribes of southern California and those along the Nevada border relied heavily on the piñon pine (*Pinus cembroides*). The Washoe spent their winters in the Reno area, then migrated up into the Sierra to hunt and harvest the piñon. For the Washoe, harvest was called *gumsaba,* or "big time," and they could gather ten thousand pounds of nuts in a good year. For the Cahuilla, Panamints, and other Great Basin tribes, the piñon represented the most important food source, but many suffered toward the end of winter because the nuts did not store nearly as long as the acorn or the mesquite bean. Famine was a frequent specter among desert tribes with heavy reliance on piñon, for, as with all plants, the production of seed can vary with annual weather patterns.

The groves were so essential they were considered sacred, and gathering was done carefully so as not to damage tree limbs. Each year the Indians thanked the trees and the earth for its bounty by planting water-saturated cones to encourage more trees. There were other types of pines, such as the sugar pine (*Pinus lambertiana*), that also lived in the same high-elevation ecosystem as the piñon, and these nuts were collected as well. All were extracted and prepared much the same way as those of the digger pine.

Manzanitas
Arctostaphylos spp.

There are over thirty different species of manzanitas native to various parts of California. They can be found as ground-hugging mats along the coast, to tree-sized shrubs in the digger pine belt of the Sierra. One species even grows in the inhospitable high-mountain ranges, but there it is stunted by heavy snowfall. There is much interest in manzanitas as landscape plants, but they prove uncooperative because native conditions consist of fast-draining, marginally fertile soil which remains completely dry much of the year.

Most manzanitas have a similar deep-red bark, and some species experience an annual peeling, where it rolls off the trunk in curled, paper-thin sheets. The sinuous growth habit makes the branching structure highly ornamental. Leaves are generally stiff and range from lime green to an almost blue-gray depending on the species. A member of the heath family, which also includes heather, manzanita bears the same small, urn-shaped, pink or white flowers. They appear early in spring in tiny clusters of pendulous, dainty bells, developing into similarly sized red berries during summer. These stiff, waxy blossoms are so filled with nectar, the scent and taste of honey is profound after chewing an entire fresh flower. The manzanita fruit matures quickly and is succulent for only a short time before its flesh becomes mealy and practically all seed.

The manzanita was an important plant to many Native California tribes, but it was noticed by the Spanish as well, who dubbed it *manzanita,* or "little apple." It was also a favored food of bears, and one of the species is *uva-ursi,* commonly called bearberry. The tribes that relied most heavily on manzanita were those of the Sierra and coastal mountain ranges, where the plant attains significant proportions and grows densely in the chaparral. Celebrations and dancing surrounded the gathering of ripe berries, a time the Concows called the "big eat." However, there are numerous reports that ingestion of too many manzanita berries caused serious bowel problems and sometimes death.

Berries were made into a refreshing summer cider. The Yuki tribes also fermented the cider for vinegar as well as a mildly alcoholic beverage. The cider was made using the entire berry, or only the flesh exclusive of the seed. It was ground into meal and allowed to steep in water, which was then strained off into a watertight basket. It would keep from two to four days without souring. At social gatherings the Indians would dip certain grasses or hawk feathers into a community pot of cider and suck the juice from them. The acidity of the berries also made them a popular source of jelly flavoring for miners' wives and others isolated in the northern California backcountry. The jelly is still popular.

The Indians also made a strong tea of manzanita leaves as a treatment for poison oak. They were known to smoke dried leaves in lieu of tobacco. The older women of the Concow tribe would chew the leaves into a thick mass and place this on sores of humans and animals to speed healing. Today leaves of the *uva-ursi* species can be found at most herb stores. It is a well-known medicinal for urinary tract infections and also contains diuretic properties. However, this is not a safe medicinal, as it can be quite toxic if ingested in overly large quantities.

Manzanita is also one of the "gasoline" plants of the California chaparral: It is so loaded with volatile oils, the leaves literally glow under the right combinations of moonlight and moisture. Its wood burns nearly as hot as coal, and embers last for such a long time that white settlers often employed manzanita in blacksmiths' forges. It has also been responsible for chimney fires of less informed residents. Whole plants, even when the foliage is green and alive, will burst into flame if touched off. It is understandable why firefighters have such a difficult time controlling wildfires in this type of vegetation.

During the nineteenth century there was a perpetual search for a perfectly straight, yard-long branch of manzanita—an entertaining challenge inspired by its gnarled growth habit. Visitors from the East commonly brought home manzanita canes, sinuous examples of this curiosity from the West. (For detailed information on the habits and distribution of native manzanitas, consult Lester Rowntree's book *Flowering Shrubs of California.* Although long out of print, there is a copy in practically every library in California.)

The Yuccas
Yucca spp.

There are different species of yucca native to the deserts of southeastern California, and some will even grow in certain coastal ranges. The most readily identified is the very large Joshua tree (*Yucca*

California Wildfires

To define the ecosystems of California in their truly pristine states would require us to go back before humans inhabited North America. With Native Americans prior to European contact, California was actually a well-managed landscape. They were active in altering their environment to improve the availability of food as well as the production of raw materials for crafts and implements. Their primary tool was fire, and reports of widespread Indian burning have been recorded in the accounts of early Spanish explorers. Today more detailed studies by ethnobotanists have proven that this land management indeed occurred, but in more deliberate and varied techniques than first thought.

Native American men were primarily concerned with hunting game, and they burned to improve access in the often dense chaparral, but also because newly scorched ground tended to yield an abundance of grasses. This in turn attracted herbivores large and small, reducing the hunters' need to travel far to obtain fresh meat. The women also burned to improve their food supply, but more importantly they directly used fire to manipulate native plants to produce more abundant seed crops and raw materials better suited to basket making. Because a great number of baskets were used for so many different purposes, obtaining the fibers was always of primary importance.

Fire eliminated the accumulation of chaff beneath oak tree canopies, making it much easier to gather the acorns. The new grass throughout the countryside benefited from the ash and produced much more generous seed heads. Having evolved to withstand periodic fire, shrubs of the chaparral sprang up with renewed vigor from the gnarled underground roots after the trunk and limbs were burned away. These new, rank suckers of many chaparral species were valuable materials for baskets since they were of even diameter, lacking in side branches, and very long. Sometimes a large pile of flammable materials was stacked around an old redbud, then set aflame. This eliminated the woody part; the following season, desired suckering would result.

The California landscape was much different from today's ecosystems because of frequent low-intensity fires. The chaparral was open, forest trees widely spaced, and the oak woodlands more extensive. Today these same ecosystems are crowded with vegetation from a century of fire suppression. Neither natural fires nor those of the Indians have been allowed to burn. These wildlands are not particularly healthy, as the competition for the little soil moisture and nutrients is keen, and now when fires burn they char every living thing in their paths. We have altered this landscape, transforming it from that under the wise Native Americans' management to one under relative non-management, and thus our most beautiful forests are at risk.

Anyone wishing to learn more about the fascinating methods of vegetation management and horticulture practiced by California tribes should read *Before the Wilderness: Environmental Management by Native Californians*, a collection of papers on the subject compiled and edited by Thomas C. Blackburn and Kat Anderson. It is very informative, essential reading, with detailed reports on how the Indians used fire, coppicing, propagation, and other techniques to make native vegetation produce more abundantly.

brevifolia), which provides habitat for many types of wildlife due to its size, which may reach as much as thirty feet tall. In the Joshua Tree National Monument, these great plants grow like a forest of distorted conifers.

The tree originally obtained its name from Mormon settlers. In 1857 a colony of Mormons in San Bernardino was asked to migrate through the desert and into Utah, where the center of the religion had been established by Brigham Young. The immigrants left the Los Angeles basin through the Cajon Pass and into the yucca forests of the Mohave Desert. There they found the arms of these great plants much like those of a Biblical prophet pointing out the way to the promised land. Since the natural range of *Yucca brevifolia* follows the way northeast through various deserts toward Utah, the Mormons believed its presence to be a sign that the heavens guided their journey. Hence, they fondly named the distorted trees after their favorite prophet, Joshua.

This yucca has been exploited in the past and fortunately is now well protected. But in the late 1800s the fibrous pulp of the trees was deemed suitable for making paper, and an English company went so far as to establish a mill at Ravenna in Soledad Pass. It is said that several editions of a London journal were printed upon yucca fiber paper, but the cost of manufacture eliminated its use. The wood is curious, as it bends easily in one direction but is unyielding in the other, a quality which led surgeons to prefer it as a lightweight splinting material. This feature was also useful to orchard farmers, who could bend slabs of Joshua tree wood around the bases of their saplings to discourage rabbits from gnawing on the soft young bark of fruit tree saplings.

At the end of the nineteenth century, Los Angeles became a mecca for health-seekers and others wishing to relocate to the mild climate. Land speculation and fantastic real estate deals were developed to take advantage of this new interest in the region. Perhaps the most bizarre scheme concerned the Joshua trees that were plentiful on the site of a proposed Mohave Desert community called Widneyville-by-the-Desert.

At that time the orange, with its bright fruit and highly fragrant flowers, was considered the ultimate symbol of Western luxury, richness, and elegance. Wily developers knew many of their prospective buyers hailed from the Eastern states and had little if any knowledge of orange trees. Gathering up their laborers and crates of cheap

𝓜ohave Desert yucca (*Yucca schidigera*). (*California State Library*)

oranges, the promoters fanned out in the project area to trim off the dried leaves of the Joshua trees. They then impaled the oranges upon the sharp green leaves of every yucca and the spines of cactus, so that when prospective buyers were brought to the site for a hard sell, they would find the desert abundantly laden with the most desirable fruit.

Most other species of yucca are neither tree or shrubs, but classified more as desert perennials. Yuccas all share a fibrous, bladed foliage which has long been used by Indian tribes as material for building and weaving. It is often confused with its relative the more succulent agave, as both have the bladelike foliage with sharp tips or thorns, but these are very different plants.

The yucca reproduces by large candles of creamy white blossoms, which maintain a unique relationship with certain species of moth. The flowers are open during the daytime and visited by bees and other insects, which, however, do not carry on pollination, as the blooms are nyctitropic. This botanical term indicates there is a change which occurs at nightfall. During the day the cuplike blossoms hang downward, but at dusk the yucca flowers turn to face the sky to emit their fragrance. This artificial pheromone, or sexual scent, attracts the yucca moths (*Tegeticula yuccasella*), although different species of moth may be required for specific types of yucca.

Yuccas usually need to crosspollinate with another plant to set seed. Due to the unique, heavy nature of its pollen, the yucca would not be capable of pollination without the assistance of these moths. The moth not only picks up this rather heavy, moist pollen but rolls it into a ball as well. She carries the ball to another yucca plant, where she lays her eggs deep inside the flower and plugs the hole with the pollen ball. Her offspring will hatch and feed upon the flower's developing ovary, but always leaving a sufficient number of seeds behind to sustain the species.

The many species of yucca provided an essential source of food and materials for the desert tribes. Its roots contained saponifying properties; even after detergents were available, the people of the desert still preferred yucca root shampoo for making their black hair lustrous. The stems of yucca were cut into round slices, then beaten with a rock or club to yield a pulp used for washing. The fibrous leaves were twisted into baskets, netting, rope, and even bowstrings.

The Cahuilla of the Mohave extracted a soft but durable fiber from the native Mohave yucca (*Yucca schidigera*). The leaves were soaked and worked until the pulp was stripped off; the resulting fibers were buried in mud to be whitened. Once cleaned, they were carefully combed, then woven or braided. Many other desert tribes also used the yucca fibers, most often to make heavy-soled sandals. Yucca fiber is unique in being both long-lasting and soft to the touch. Vaqueros of early California highly prized the saddle blankets woven by Indians from yucca fiber. These were soft and allowed a better exchange of air between the saddle and a horse's back than wool or cotton, thereby reducing the prevalent sores, which could put the animal out of work until they healed. The small blankets were woven on a primitive loom and decorated with contrasting patterns by dye from the roots of the Joshua tree.

The yucca also provided the Indians with an important food in their dry desert environment. Yucca seedpods can measure up to five inches long and are quite edible. While green and unripe, they were roasted in coals. The flower stalk of our Lord's candle (*Yucca whipplei*), is profoundly beautiful, with each stalk containing thousands of pure white bells. Unfortunately, this yucca dies after flowering and setting seed, leaving the barren spikes standing rigid like skeleton sentinels of the desert. The flowers, when nearing maturity, were cut before flowering and roasted to yield a very sweet, soft pulp, which some say resembles the flavor of baked apples. The flowers were also eaten raw when still young and tender. Early ranchers often resorted to feeding these parts of the yucca to their livestock during drought.

The Agaves
Agave spp.

The agave is related to the yucca, but only one well-known species, *Agave deserti*, is a California native from the Colorado Desert of California. The other species originate in other southwestern states, Mexico, and the Mediterranean. Native American tribes used the plants interchangeably for many uses. Rigid, blue *Agave americana* and the softer *Agave attenuata* are both popular landscape plants, but they were not necessarily used by our tribes except after introduction of the former to the mission system.

Agave provides important fibers to many nations around the world which cultivate these plants of the Americas. Because this is an easily propagated, shallow-rooted plant, it is often the only species capable of surviving thin or rocky soils as well as prolonged dry seasons and intense heat. The fibrous product rendered from the fleshy leaves, sisal, was widely used by southwestern Native American tribes for weaving, ropes, and lashing. The California vaqueros first used only braided calfhide reatas to work their cattle from horseback. As the cattle industry changed, the old reatas yielded to ropes of twisted agave fibers, similar to those used by cowboys today.

Various methods were used to prepare agave fibers, since they were buried within the fleshy leaves. Leaves were soaked in water until the pulp rotted off, in a method similar to that used with yucca. Sometimes the leaves were dried out, then beaten to loosen the fibers. Agave fiber was twisted into cords by rolling with the hand across a bare thigh. The incredibly strong finished product was used for bow strings, carrying nets, and hammocks. Combs and brushes were also fashioned from the stiffer fibers. Agave was also burned, the resulting charcoal used as coloring in tattoos, the skin pricking done with the very sharp thorns of prickly pear or cholla.

Agave deserti, our native species, is also a food plant. Its interesting life cycle is key to its common name, century plant, as it requires about fifteen years to store enough energy to bloom. Its efforts produce an incredibly tall bloom spike, which can vary from about ten to twenty-five feet tall and may be well over a foot thick at the base. In most species the original plant dies after blooming. However, the clumping growth habit tends to produce plenty of "pups," or suckers, at the base of the mother plant, which later mature after the original has bloomed and died.

Although the spikes are an incredible wonder, they lack the spectacular flowers of the yucca and its complex pollination requirements. Mexicans today harvest the agave, which they call "mescal." The developing bloom spike is cut off, and the sweet sap from the stump is collected and fermented into tequila and the less well-known *pulque*. It is of interest to note the California tribes never made these alcoholic drinks as did the Apache, using the plant strictly for food and fiber.

In April southern California tribes, notably the Cahuilla, harvest the bloom stalks while they are still fresh and roast them. The flowers are eaten as well. The roots, as with the yucca, contain soap. Agave gathering is done in groups, followed by a celebration where the mescal heads at the center of the agave are cooked into a sweet delicacy. The stalks and leaves are cut away, and the heads are dropped into a pit in the sand lined with hot stones. They are covered with grass, then buried beneath the ground to cook for a few days. When completed, the result is a sticky, molasseslike mass. For people who relied on plants for most of their food, imagine the delight of these harvests, with the leaves reserved for fibers, the heart of the plant cooked for a feast, and the spikes carried home to store for future use.

Only two agaves are often found in California gardens, although more obscure species frequently appear in botanical collections. *Agave americana*, the true century plant, is relatively frost-tolerant. It is very large, with its stiff blue leaves reaching sometimes over five feet tall, the edges barbed with vicious thorns. There is evidence that this plant, like the prickly pear, was planted as a living fence on ranchos and mission sites, and throughout the Southwest it is one of a handful of plants that most typify Western gardens. In dry landscapes consisting mostly of packed, unplanted earth, older stands of agave develop into dramatic clusters, with the mother plants surrounded by many pups at their bases. A mother original plant may grow into a mound ten to twenty feet in diameter before it finally blooms and dies. Later, as the many offspring take its place and also mature, they may simultaneously send up their massive bloom spikes for an incredible display.

Agave attenuata is far more tender and succulent, restricted to the light-frost portions of the south coast. It is a more tropical-appearing species, the leaves light green, and sharp only at each tip. They do not develop such large clusters, and the "cabbages" of leaves are often facing at an angle, rather than straight up as with the desert agaves. The most wonderful quality is the bloom, which does not grow straight up but outward and drooping like a massive elephant trunk. It is literally sheathed in blooms, rather than displaying the telephone pole candelabra of the rigid agaves.

The Daturas
Brugmansia hybrids, *Datura suavolens*

Datura, a broad-leafed weed native to most parts of the United States, is known variously as jimsonweed, angel's trumpet, thorn apple, locoweed, toloache, and main-oph-weep. It bears unusually large, white, trumpet-shaped flowers succeeded by prickly seedpods about the size of golf balls. The first recorded event concerning datura occurred during the 1676 rebellion in the Jamestown Colony. As well documented by Robert Beverly in 1705, English soldiers stationed in the colony, believing that the leaves of the datura made suitable pot greens, boiled a mess of them up and consumed the lot. The result was that the soldiers turned "natural Fools" and "in this Frantic Condition they were confined, lest they should in their Folly destroy themselves; though it was observed that all their Actions were full of Innocence and good Nature." The effects lasted for eleven days before the soldiers returned to their senses.

In the West, datura was well known to many tribes, particularly those in southern California and other southwestern states. Authorities suggest its use in religious ritual originated in Latin America and gradually spread northward. Most religions of the California tribes fall into one of two basic categories: shamanism,

The native plant known as jimsonweed, with its seedpods and smaller white flowers.

which was more prevalent in the northern tribes, and the cult of toloache in the south. Toloache is based primarily on using datura as a hallucinogenic drug to induce a dreamlike state, during which visions were experienced. The images seen in these hallucinations were the base from which an individual's place in the natural world was interpreted, thus defining his or her personal spirituality. It is believed that this jimsonweed cult, or toloache, originated with the Aztecs and gradually moved northward from Mexico into the desert southwest, which explains why use of datura was not common in tribes north of central California.

Datura is a member of the nightshade family (Solanaceae) along with deadly nightshade, mandrake, foxglove, and henbane. All nightshades contain highly poisonous alkaloids (although fruits of some members, such as tomatoes and eggplants, are edible). It is thought the toloache cults gained momentum after the establishment of the missions because the Catholic teaching caused more subtle aspects of traditional Native American spirituality and beliefs to become neglected. As a result, datura use increased in the same tribes that also accepted Christianity, and in some cases toloache use moved northward into many new tribal units during the late 1700s and early 1800s.

The potency of datura also interested early physicians; like with other medicinals, there is a fine line between dosages that cure and those that kill. During the nineteenth century, datura, medicinally termed *stramonium*, provided a very effective treatment for asthma. Since ingestion of the plant was so dangerous, asthma powders were prepared that mixed dried leaves with saltpeter. The mix was ignited and the resulting smoke inhaled. In some cases, the datura leaves were rolled with other herbs into medicinal cigarettes. The active ingredients contained in the plant are primarily hyoscine, atropine, and hyoscyamine. An overdose is characterized by a talkative delirium termed by nineteenth-century physicians as the "belladonna jag." It must be said that the chemicals in datura, like those in foxglove, can be absorbed through the skin, and just brushing against the wild species can cause rashes.

Today this annual weed still dots the California countryside, but more attractive perennial hybrids and imported South American species are cultivated in southern gardens. The botanical nomenclature has changed over the years, and the genus *Datura* has been changed to *Brugmansia*. Ornamental daturas are generally quite frost-tender and restricted to coastal gardens, where they bloom prolifically. But they do take quite well to pots and may be grown in cooler climates if protected, or moved indoors during frosts. Plants are not particularly attractive when not in bloom and should be cut back after flowering to encourage a more compact branching habit. In fact, creative pruning can result in absolutely stunning specimens.

The flowers of *Brugmansia candida* bloom in very large, pale white trumpets that hang pendulously in gangly shrubs, which may grow well over ten feet tall. The flowers open in the afternoon and are said to literally glow in the moonlight. *Brugmansia sanguinia* and other South American species produce especially showy, bright pink and red trumpets. Datura, one of the most neglected Western plants, should be resurrected not only for its role in our history but for the sheer beauty of its blooms.

California Bay
Umbellularia californica

The European relative of California bay is known as sweet bay or Grecian laurel. The ancient Greeks placed a wreath of sweet bay upon the heads of their greatest warriors and athletes as a sign of victory. The dried leaves from this Mediterranean plant are sold as culinary bay leaves.

California bay is native to foothill regions of both California and Oregon. It is a shrubby evergreen that eventually reaches treelike proportions. The leaves are potently scented with oil that makes them unattractive to insects. The pioneers used the wild bay leaves in their pantries to discourage weevils, which would quickly spoil dry foods in the warmer months. Even today in these transitional belts where the tree grows, people insert freshly picked California bay leaves into their flour bags and jars. The leaves may be substituted for sweet bay in cooking, and the native is said to impart far more flavor than the traditional variety. The Indians also made similar use of the foliage, scattering leaves in their huts to control fleas. Just as eucalyptus oil is enjoyed by steamroom connoisseurs, the California Indians crushed bay leaves to scent their skin in sweat lodges.

One common name for this plant is myrtlewood, a name alluding to the beauty of wood milled from bay trees. It is dense, heavy, and richly tinted with a multicolored swirling grain. During the nineteenth century it was preferred for small, high-stress fittings of ships due to its great strength. The more attractive qualities were sought after by furniture makers, and today West Coast craftsmen are redis-covering interest in myrtlewood for a variety of handmade items, such as bowls and beads. The California bay also makes an excellent landscape plant, best used as a reliable, drought-tolerant background shrub or tree.

Shrubs of the Chaparral

Many foothill regions of California are cloaked in dense chap-arral, which is made up of trees, shrubs, and perennials. The chapar-ral tends to become dominant on sloping, fast-draining hills with less than fertile soil. It occurs at specific elevations, from a few hundred feet, where the grassy oak woodlands end, and extends to the lower reaches of the pine forests. From this plant community come some of our most promising natives for landscaping, shrubs which also played important roles in the cultures of Native Americans who once popu-lated the foothills.

Two of the most well-documented northern California tribes are the Maidu and Miwok, who inhabited large tracts on the western slopes of the Sierra Nevada. Ishi, the lone survivor of the neighboring Yahi, was discovered in the early twentieth century living as his ances-tors did. He and other small groups clinging to the old ways shared their knowledge of plants with early ethnologists. Therefore, much of the information we have about chaparral plants is based on these cul-tures, although other tribes no doubt understood their value as well. Manzanita, discussed elsewhere, was a unique plant and the domi-nant species of many chaparral belts. The three other flowering shrubs which are both prevalent and of landscape value include California lilac and toyon, which are evergreen, and redbud, which is deciduous.

There are about as many different native species of *Ceanothus* as there are manzanitas. California lilac is also an evergreen shrub that varies widely in form, from low mats to uprights of nearly treelike proportions. California lilac has become wildly popular of late as a landscape plant for its many shades of vivid blue, violet, and even white flowers. However, it was of greater interest to British gardeners earlier in this century, when they developed a number of excellent hybrids that are now in cultivation in the United States. California lilac continues to confound gardeners with rather finicky roots that abhor wet soil. But given a small rise in the ground plain, a southern exposure, and plenty of heat, california lilac will bloom profusely each spring with absolutely no care.

Indians used California lilac only to a limited extent, preferring the strong branch wood for arrow shafts and digging implements. The plant's most important quality was the saponifiers in its flowers, which served as a shampoo. Although the soaproot bulb was also plentiful, it required laborious digging and preparation, while ceanothus blossoms could be simply stripped from their branches and crushed between the palms in a nearby stream to create lather. Its bark was also made into tea for medicinal purposes.

Ceanothus thyrsiflorus was the first of the California species recognized, discovered by J.F. Eschscholz on an expedition in 1815 which passed through the San Francisco Bay area. (He was also the first botanist to describe and name the California poppy, whose genus bears his name.) This ceanothus grew in dense tickets on the coastal hills and was grubbed out to build houses there. But its blooms were so lovely, settlers often left larger specimens to beautify their modest dwellings. There are older references to ceanothus thickets, suggesting cowboys wore chaps to protect their legs from these branches, which were made prickly by the many fine but very stiff twigs.

The stems of western redbud (*Cercis occidentalis*) provided a primary material for basket cores among a large number of California tribes. It was also traded with tribes whose lands did not contain redbuds, which created a persistent demand. To encourage wild plants to produce sufficient material for their needs, and to insure it grew to the desired thickness, favorite shrubs were burned. The flames consumed the woody trunks and branches; the following spring the plant would sprout up from the root crown with perfectly sized whips. Later on, after fire prevention was encouraged by settlers, the Indians coppiced redbuds. This horticultural term describes methods of pruning that encourage quantities of suckerlike growth for harvest. These were among the unique horticultural practices whereby Native Californians preserved wild plants as sources of food and raw materials.

The light red coloring in redbud bark was preferred as material for contrasts in basket patterns. To intensify the color, segments of stripped bark were exposed to smoke or a soaking in water containing wood ashes. Rust-colored tinting was sometimes achieved by soaking redbud bark strips in a tea of oak bark and scraps of old iron.

Long whips of rank-growing younger plants were preferred over stiff, twiggy, closely spaced joints of old wood. Each whip was split into three segments, then stored for future use.

Another report tells us that the early settlers in California used the bark of redbud as a substitute for quinine when suffering from the chills and fever of malaria. With the vast Central Valley wetlands intact, there was considerable difficulty with malaria in the early days, due to hordes of mosquitoes.

Western redbud is by far the showiest plant in the foothills, standing out clearly from the surrounding vegetation. It is bare for the winter months, but early in spring nearly every part of it is shrouded in tiny, pea-shaped, magenta-purple flowers—a reminder that it is an unlikely member of the legume family. Once the flowers fade, the foliage appears, each leaf heart-shaped. In late summer the leaves move toward dormancy, not from the cold nights of autumn but by another mechanism, perhaps dryness. The fall colors of redbud are quite brilliant, ranging from a deep, smoky pink to bright yellow. Close inspection reveals unusual combinations of colors on a single leaf unlike that of any other plant in California.

Redbud has proven to be most forgiving of cultivated gardens and will adapt to any location, provided the drainage is reasonable. Naturally occurring redbud may resent supplemental watering during the dry months, as it is unaccustomed to the moisture. Nursery-grown seedlings, which are watered regularly from the start, tend to grow much faster than wild plants. It is best to buy these container-grown seedlings or start plants at home from seed rather than attempt to transplant wild seedlings. Redbud is one of our finest xeriscape gardening plants, offering all the color and variety of traditional shrubs with the incredible endurance of a native.

Throughout the Sierra winters, toyon (*Heteromeles arbutifolia*) shrubs are laden with bunches of bright red berries, a welcome source of color when the oaks stand bare and the brown grass has laid down from the rain. Early settlers found its fruit timely for the Nativity and named it Christmas berry, or California holly, just as the white spirea blooms in May and was thus dubbed bridal wreath. Victorian florists of California combined the prickly, hollylike leaves of evergreen coast live oak with sprays of these red berries to resemble the true hollies so popular in the East.

This vigorous evergreen shrub is one of the most promising for drought-tolerant gardening because it will grow under the very driest conditions. Plants provide solid greenery, which may also be sheared or pruned to informal hedges to increase the density of foliage. It is so rugged, in fact, that chaparral land cleared by dozers quickly sprouts green branches from the sheared-off stumps of older plants. This proves it is nearly impossible to kill the plant, except with perpetually soggy ground.

The Indians used toyon primarily as a food plant. The berries were of greater value because they matured during a season when other botanical foods were unavailable. For immediate use, the berries were placed next to hot coals and parched. Another method cooked them under constant heat for up to three days in a pit oven. A long-term method of preparation was simply to store them for a few months in baskets until they softened.

PLANTS AND BASKET MAKING

The single most noteworthy craft of the California tribes is their proficiency at basket making. Although a few tribes in the southeastern corner of the state did use pottery, it had its limitations. Heavy, fragile, and unwieldy when gathering lightweight materials such as seeds, pottery did not promise any improvement in the material culture and lifestyles of most California tribes. Museum specimens show the care and workmanship Native American women gave to the creation of each basket, and the mere fact they survive today in good condition attests to their durability.

It is worth a visit to any of California's fine history museums to fully appreciate the workmanship of these baskets in detail. At the California Native American Museum at Sutter's Fort is a collection of unique ornamental baskets decorated in colorful feather down and beads; some miniature examples have stitching so small as to be nearly invisible. At the Indian Museum in the Yosemite Valley, you can see actual demonstrations of Miwok skills from basket weaving to acorn preparation.

We all tend to visualize California Indian baskets as tightly coiled bowls, but this represents only one of many styles. Coiled baskets utilized a core material of split willow or redbud that was sown into a basket with perfectly spaced stitches. A sharp deer-bone awl was generally required to force holes between coils for the stitches; desert tribes preferred the thorn of prickly pear cactus, set into a hard

Collection of California Native American baskets, including a cradleboard, cooking baskets, winnowing trays, and seed beaters, exhibiting the wide variety of patterns and shapes which were finely crafted by women. (*California State Library*)

piece of asphaltum, then wrapped in hide. The Maidu and Miwok used coiling for their watertight cooking baskets, and this became the preferred method for a family's decorative basketware reserved for ceremonial purposes. Another method called twining arranges the warp into a number of stays radiating from the center at the base of the basket. A weft of twisted grass was woven in and out of these stays with the fingertips, requiring no awl. If patterns were used, the grass was overlaid but not replaced with colored material. The result was a more quickly made utility basket with thinner walls that proved more flexible and lightweight than a coiled basket.

Unique to the southern California tribes was the addition of naturally occurring asphaltum to make their baskets watertight.

There is a story of an Indian woman who was abandoned on the Island of San Nicolas, one of the Channel Islands off the California coast, after the rest of her tribe was forced back to the mainland by the Spanish. It is said that fifteen years later she was found still living on the island, making waterproof baskets. She is recorded to have done this by placing lumps of asphalt tar into a basket with hot rocks and rolling them around until the tar melted and evenly coated the inside. This practice was found among eastern California tribes of Shoshone blood as well.

In the Sierra Nevada where soaproot (*Chloragalum pertidinum*) was plentiful, its mucilaginous flesh was worked into the inside niches of a finished gathering or burden basket. This sealed it, preventing the smaller seeds from working into the weaving and either leaking out the bottom or creating new holes. Soaproot is an essential plant, and its outer, fibrous husk was made into quite durable brushes by various Sierra tribes. These were in such great demand, they were traded to many others whose lands did not contain the bulbous plant.

The inside scales of the soaproot bulb are succulent, with snow white flesh. This provided glue, as indicated above, but more importantly made a high-quality soap when peeled and grated on a rigid sifting basket. My own backyard test proved to me the soap was not only simple to harvest but produced considerable suds. No wonder some Indian women continued to use soaproot as shampoo long after commercial detergents became available.

But basket making was not limited to just fashioning containers. Rigid materials were constructed more coarsely into open sifters for food preparation, notably the processing of acorns. Most tribes wove a lightweight, paddle-shaped tool, much like a badminton racket, called a seed beater, which helped to tap wild grains from their seed heads directly into a basket held below. With these same rigid willow strips, a mother would weave a cradleboard to carry her baby on her back, leaving her

Old botanical drawing of the soaproot bulb and its tall flower stalk. Most aboveground portions of the plant completely die back early, and the bulbs become dormant for most of the summer.

The Versatile Cattail

Wherever there is water, along riverbanks, in poorly drained ground, and at the margins of ponds or lakes, there will always be the cattail. Its distinctive, cigar-shaped seed heads stand out among other grasses and sedges of the marsh. When mature, the seed head disintegrates into tufts of cottony fibers called cattail down, which helps the seed travel on the wind. If the fibers land upon moist ground or water, which give the preferred conditions for germination, they collapse, ensuring the seed remains there to sprout.

Cradleboards were used by practically every tribe throughout the state to bind and carry a baby safely on the mother's back while her hands remained free to work. Diapers as we know them were not part of the material culture, but a mother would pack this cattail down, a very absorbent material, around the child's body. It could be arranged easily, then held in place by wrapping the child and tying him or her securely to the cradleboard. The soiled material was later discarded; with the wide distribution of cattail reeds, it was a simple matter to obtain more.

The down was also used later in the nineteenth century for stuffing furniture, and it could be woven or even twisted into fibers used in burlap and other webbing material. The soft down was also pressed into an excellent insulation for both deadening sound and reducing heat loss, which could make it an environmentally friendly alternative to fiberglass. Down was also used as a caulking material between stays of wood barrels.

The seed head itself, if harvested before disintegration, is neatly packed into a dense, cigar-shaped mass. This is an excellent stage for storing what would later become a bulky material if the fibers detached and puffed up. Early settlers discovered the large hollow stems of the seed stalks made perfect disposable candle molds, because the fibrous material could be peeled away easily from the hardened candle wax. People also used the entire bloom stalk for a torch when the seed and down were still immature and in tightly consolidated form. The stalk was cut and the end dipped in coal oil, then set aflame.

Virtually every part of the cattail plant is edible. The male flowers are cooked green, like corn on the cob, while only the soft center of the female flowers is preferred. Young shoots collected in spring can be peeled and eaten as asparagus, either boiled or raw.

The roots are rich in starch and may be scraped clean of husks, dried and eaten raw, or grated and boiled as a vegetable. Many Native American tribes dried and pounded the roots, combining them with cattail pollen to yield a flour used to make bread, pudding, and, later on, pancakes. The roots also contain plentiful sugars and were boiled down into syrup. Some believe the nutrient value of cattail root is similar to that of corn or rice, an important fact considering the plant grows like a weed in soggy wastes and is virtually maintenance-free. This was proven during World War I, when the German people faced starvation but found an unexpected food source in cattail flour. After winnowing off the down, even the seeds can be ground into meal, which is combined with other staple foods.

To some, cattails represent a new, yet old, food source that can be of great value in developing countries. Plant scientists have tested the cattail and found that plants can be cultivated using certain methods to make them far more productive. One acre of cattails planted for the starchy roots produced approximately ten times the harvest of the same area planted to potatoes. The expected yield of cattail root averaged 140 tons per acre. And as if this were not enough, researchers have fermented the flour to produce ethyl alcohol.

hands free for gathering. The northeastern tribes relied heavily on fishing for their staple food, and cordage of basket material was woven into ingenious nets and fish traps. A flexible, softer network was also used as backing for aprons and capes of feathers, or decorated with other attractive materials.

The plants chosen for basket making varied with the ecosystems where the tribes lived. In the majority of cases, willow proved to be the most universal material, prepared in a variety of ways for both warp and weft. In the Central Valley, various reeds or tules were combined with willow core materials. Foothill tribes relied heavily on western redbud, willow, big-leaf maple, and dogwood. Desert tribes used the fibers of the native fan palm.

Certain plants were used to provide color and pattern to the baskets. Some dyed basic materials such as cattail leaves. In place of the basic materials, others were used, the most interesting of which is the maidenhair fern (*Adiantum jordanii*). A close look at this dainty-leaved fern reveals jet black stems as shiny as though they had been polished. They closely resemble black plastic lanyards. The inside of redbud bark, a strong red color, was the primary accent material of mountain tribes. There are also examples of small porcupine quills flattened and dyed, then worked into the baskets, just as plains tribes used prepared quills to decorate their clothing before the introduction of trade beads.

It is important to note that the Indians did not simply pick the basket weaving materials and immediately put them to use. In the case of the redbud and many other plants, the bark could be stripped only in the early spring when the sap was rising, and only from twigs of a certain age. Therefore, coppiced plants were of great value and were managed carefully in order to produce greater quantities of the desired whips. Grasslike plants were gathered only during certain seasons when the fibers were at the right stage of growth. It was not uncommon for harvests of basket materials to be followed by long periods of preparation while the wood was still green and supple. This was no small task when the only available woodworking tools were obsidian points, antler bone, and cactus spines.

Because the California tribes are so diverse, each unit relied on a slightly different group of plants for its basketwork. Some of the most common have already been mentioned, but grasses such as tule (*Scirpus acutus*), common cattail, and a variety of sedges were of particular importance to valley tribes, which did not have access to chaparral plant materials. Other basket making materials include bear grass (*Xerophyllum tenax*), dyed for decorative overlay; pines (*Pinus* spp.), whose roots provide color and whose pitch is a sealant; squaw bush (*Rhus trilobata*), used in coils and wrapping; California lilac (*Ceanothus cuneatus*), for stiffening; and desert fan palm (*Washingtonia robusta*), for its fronds.

NOTEWORTHY WILDFLOWERS

The diversity of wildflowers in California is nearly as great as that of our Native American tribes. But the California poppy and lupine are the most easily recognized as symbols of the Far West. Our golden yellow poppy (*Eschscholzia californica*) extends the length and breadth of the state and tends to develop large colonies where growing conditions are ideal. When some early Spanish explorers first saw the southern California coastal hills cloaked in orange blooms, they were inspired to name them *Tierra del Fuego*: the land of fire. Upon close inspection of the flowers themselves, the shape and brilliancy inspired the name *copa de oro*.

Despite its unusual genus name, the California poppy is a member of the true poppy family. As a result, it contains scant traces of the same alkaloids as the opium poppy. Yet another Spanish name, *dormidera* (from *dormir*, "to sleep"), attested to the plant's mildly narcotic properties and Indians found some relief in placing the root beside a sore tooth. Apparently the plants were also cooked down into a more potent tea to remedy insomnia and headaches. It is thought that the women sometimes used it to encourage unresponsive lovers by offering the drink disguised in some other form. It seems to have been somewhat effective, for if her act was discovered by others in the tribe, she would be expelled.

The California poppy blooms once in spring and is actually a short lived perennial often treated as an annual. An individual may persist for a number of years if conditions are suitable.

The blue flower spikes of the lupine are nearly as familiar as the poppy, and these plants are often found growing together. Yet some naturally occurring stands of lupine display creamy yellow or pinkish flowers, as well. There are many different species of lupines in California, some perennial, upright, woody plants, while a good number of them are annual.

The fact that lupines are legumes is proven by the pealike shape of each small flower. Like clovers, lupines are also capable of transferring atmospheric nitrogen into the soil to improve fertility. Strangely, its botanical genus name is derived from *lupus*, or "wolf," as it was thought to rob the soil of its nutrients. This belief originated in the fact that lupines, like other species of legume, are the first to appear on burn sites, where the heat has destroyed soil nitrogen. Likewise, legumes tend to predominate on well-drained soils of marginal fertility where other nonleguminous plants cannot grow for lack of nitrogen.

Lupines have no ability to reduce soil nutrients and fertility on their own. In fact, a yellow-flowering lupine was originally sown with barley on the nutritionally impoverished dunes of San Francisco. It added nitrogen and organic matter, while the roots spread out to bind the soil. This area would later become Golden Gate Park. The foliage of lupines was harvested in early spring and eaten steamed by many Native Americans, and tea was made from the leaves to treat urinary difficulties.

LESTER ROWNTREE

If you want to do a thing, make no bones about it, just do it. That's the big secret. There is no secret. It's all there for free.
LESTER ROWNTREE

Lester Rowntree (1879–1979) described herself as a "lone hunter" of California's native plants. Yet this is only a part of what made her such a unique person and so important in the world of horticulture. Her accomplishments are made more profound by the fact that she did not begin her professional life until after her divorce in 1932 at age fifty-three. She then proceeded to spend nine months out of each year traveling alone by automobile into California's most rugged backcountry to observe the native species firsthand. During the remaining three months, she lived in her cottage, perched upon a sunny hillside of Carmel overlooking the Pacific. There she wrote numerous books and articles on her views and shared this intimate knowledge of our most successful native plants for cultivated gardens.

Lester Rowntree was born Gertrude Ellen Lester in 1879 in Cumberland, England, then immigrated to the United States as a child with her family to settle in Altadena, California. Raised as a Quaker, she inherited a deep respect for nature coupled with the intrinsic British love of gardens. As a child she avidly collected flowers and seed. Her transient family later moved to Pennsylvania, where she completed high school at the age of twenty-one. She took a position as a governess, then moved home again to care for her ailing parents until they died. In 1908 she married Bernard Rowntree and bore one son, Cedric.

To truly understand Rowntree, we must look at the events of her life in historical context. Her early adult role was that of caretaker, first to her parents, then children of others, and finally for her own husband and son. Women's suffrage was in full swing during her twenties, and obtaining the vote, and later the freedoms of the roaring 1920s, had a great deal of influence on her views.

The pivotal point came in her forties, when she was diagnosed with uterine cancer and underwent surgery. Her survival was questionable, and so to enable her to see the California of her youth again before she died, the Rowntrees moved to Carmel in 1929. Fortunately, the surgery was successful. Lester went to work at various businesses with little success as her marriage failed. Finally, in 1932 she divorced and changed her name. Again, history played a part, because at that time women were not taken as seriously in scientific fields as men. Like many other aspiring professional women, Lester's maiden name became her first, probably so that her correspondence would always appear as that of a male.

With this change, she began a new life devoted to California and its unique community of plants. She set out to roam the state and well beyond its borders to study American plants wherever they occurred. Despite her advanced age for the day, Lester was not one for creature comforts and often slept in her car, even eating boiled birdseed when nothing else was available. She wandered the more rugged trails of the backcountry with a pack mule.

Over countless miles this woman studied not from a textbook or herbarium, but by observing the living plants where they occurred, how they responded to their environments, and the subtle differences between them. Hers was firsthand knowledge, an intimacy rarely experienced by academics. The seed she collected was brought back to Carmel and either planted in her garden or sold through her California native-plant seed business.

Lester's career was relatively short, as her eyesight began to fail in her seventies and her hunting days reluctantly came to a close. She remained at home in her Carmel cottage, gardening and writing a number of successful children's books. By this time Lester had become quite well known in the horticultural world, her two books on California native plants widely read and accepted. She was frequently visited by people in that field for many years. "People would ask was I afraid. I have never been afraid in my life. Fear attracts the thing you are afraid of." And so by confronting a new career at age fifty-three and continuing it for nearly twenty years, Lester proved that she was afraid of neither life nor aging. "Hell itself will yield to industry," she once wrote, and the specter of death certainly yielded before her, and only after a century of life did she finally give in.

Books by Lester Rowntree

Hardy Californians, New York: Macmillan, 1936.
Flowering Shrubs of California, Stanford California: Stanford University Press, 1939.

Honors

Honorary Secretary, British Alpine Society
Honorary President, California Native Plant Society
President-at-large, American Herb Society
National Award, American Horticultural Society

ADOBE AND
ROSES

*It is said that the first padres as they travelled up the coast
dropped mustard-seed to mark the Camino Real; and,
when the golden flowers sprang up, each in the form of a
cross, the Indians looked upon it as a miracle.*

DANE COOLIDGE
California Cowboys

The first plants to be imported into the California ecosystem came inadvertently with the early conquistadors. Their livestock, having grazed upon the pastures of Old Spain and Mexico, distributed seed across the countryside. Filaree, with its twisted needles, and parts of other weeds became entangled in the wool of Spanish sheep, then dropped off on the long drive from Mexico to California. Cattle and horses fed dried fodder in the holds of ships later aided in the distribution of seed through their manures. Early cattlemen say this greatly improved the quality of the grazing land, but contamination of the native grassland species with more competitive wild oats and foxtail has distorted many plant communities and completely replaced others.

The first outposts of Spain in California were the missions, most of which were located in the southern two-thirds of the state. It is not easy to imagine California as it was in the eighteenth century before the advent of irrigation. Much of what is now verdant farmland was a veritable desert. Rainfall was irregular, alternating between droughts and floods. But with the basic Old World skills of irrigation, the Jesuits and Franciscans were able to bring some water to their fields. Through primitive systems of reservoirs and aqueducts, the plants at missions in the dry south were able to survive the summers, except when prolonged drought dried up even the most reliable of water sources.

Due to extreme isolation, each mission had to be self-sufficient, and thus was more than simply a church to convert the Native Americans. The mission became a center of activity where many different skills were taught to the neophytes (baptized Native Californian converts) in order to assist in survival of the community. The chief contribution of the missions to California was agriculture, although the earlier gathering activities of many tribes that altered native vegetation was also a sort of farming and horticulture.

The quotation above by Dane Coolidge shows how plants played a mystical role in the ultimate purpose of the mission, to convert the Native Californians to Christianity. Another unverified story tells us that one mission community of Native Californians was divided between those who embraced Christianity by attending mass and those who refused. When planting a field, the wily padre gave those who attended mass seed potatoes with eyes, and the others just fleshy chunks of tuber. Later, when only the part of the field planted by the obedient converts sprouted, the priest claimed that God had blessed them but cursed with barren ground those less motivated to accept the new religion.

Plants were cultivated at missions for three purposes. First, agricultural crops were necessary to feed the missionaries and neophytes and to sustain livestock. Second, plants played important roles in the religious feasts of the Church, and many were grown only for their aesthetic beauty and symbolism. In addition, medicinal herbs and certain native plants with other useful properties were added to the mission grounds, the most valuable restricted to sheltered courtyards.

The missions benefited from the support of the Catholic church and the Spanish government. Plants and other necessities were brought by ship; as a result, the diversity of cultivated species at the missions was greater than in other types of early settlements. Once established, many plants were propagated, then sent along the mission chain in an organized network of trading, which often included the ranchos as well. Through this system, the diversity of agriculture

The adobe house of the Eybara family is typical of those that sprung up in Mexican California after secularization of the missions. The far end of the house shows damage where the plaster has been eroded away to reveal the adobe bricks, which are also dissolving. It is easy to see why the homesites of early California peasants lacked plantings, for water was scarce in the land of little rain. (*California State Library*)

grew rapidly and contributed to the romantic view of early California, as portrayed in Helen Hunt Jackson's 1881 novel, *Ramona*.

Life on the land grant ranchos was less industrious than at the missions, primarily because there were no armies of neophytes to do the work. The emphasis on cattle and horses was greater here, but still the people tended their kitchen gardens of corn, beans, and chiles. In the northern portion of the state, where the large rivers flowed year-round, farming was less difficult, and ambitious individuals, such as John Sutter, managed to transform their wild land grant tracts into productive farms.

Spanish homes and buildings of early California were arranged in either an L or a U shape, with a long series of rooms connected by an outdoor veranda. The resulting inner courtyard was not necessarily a paved space, but in the missions it resembled the Moorish gardens of Spain, which were usually divided formally into quadrants by walkways. These were a remnant of the Persian religious influence, where four well-defined spaces represented the quarters of the universe. In the mission courtyards, trees were planted for shading or fruit, and the space provided a quiet, contemplative dryland garden for the Franciscans. However, it was not a garden as we know today, but a dry, dusty place where the heat of the day was mitigated only by tree canopies and shadows cast by low-slung adobe buildings.

Most of the crops and orchards of the mission were planted inside a *huerta*, which was simply a fenced enclosure, whose boundaries were sometimes defined by building walls as well. Timber was scarce in many parts of coastal and southern California, so the *huerta* was most often defined by adobe brick walls. Due to the great number of available laborers, these walls could be constructed easily, but they required a cap of fired clay tiles so that rainfall would not dissolve the mud bricks. During the decline of the missions, these sites were often robbed of their building materials, with the tiles first to disappear. The loss of the caps caused these old adobe walls to literally dissolve back into the earth whence they came, leaving little behind to mark their location.

A few *huertas* did have wood or thatch fencing, but this was usually sticks and driftwood woven together into a picket or paling fence. Other materials worked into the fences included tule, palm fronds, cornstalks, and vine runners. At the mission in Santa Barbara, there is an excellent *huerta* fence reproduced in this rustic, irregular character. Another option used at the missions that can still be found in active use in rural Mexico is the living fence. Plants selected were typically agave and prickly pear because both had vicious spines and grew rather quickly. At the Leonis Adobe in Calabasas, California, remnants of an ancient prickly pear fence still exist and have grown to incredible proportions, at least twenty feet thick and equally tall, making a formidable barrier.

On the ranchos, the courtyard with buildings on two or more sides tended to be more active and sparsely planted than those of the missions. This was because the vaqueros often tied their mounts there, with a water trough and adobe ovens in the open spaces. It was considered a place of business and social gathering, and many household tasks were done in the open air of the verandas.

In most arid countries, gardening is often done in containers, as waste water can be concentrated into pots. Terra cotta pots filled with flowers and herbs decorated the verandas (and container-decorated verandas are still seen in rural Mexico today). Vines and roses were planted against pillars or posts, and only the most rugged native plants survived the beating of the hot sun in the open courtyard. Though today we often think of the Mexican hacienda with lush, colorful plantings, in reality those of early California were strictly dryland spaces. This is in part because the view of a farmer is quite different from that of a cattle rancher, who may not see the value in dragging buckets of water to plants simply because they are beautiful.

THE FLORA OF THE MISSION DAYS

The Rose

Ramona had a cloth-of-gold rose in her hand. The veranda eaves were now shaded with them, hanging down like
a thick fringe of golden tassels. It was the rose Felipe had
loved best.

Ramona
HELEN HUNT JACKSON

The Castilian rose, full and fluted, and of a chaste and
penetrating fragrance, hung singly and in clusters on the
pillars of the dwellings, on the barracks and chapel, from
the very roofs; bloomed upon bushes as high as young
trees. The Presidio was as delicately perfumed as a lady's
bower, and its cannon faced the everchanging hues of
water and island and hill.

Rezanov and Doña Concha
GERTRUDE ATHERTON

When Fra Junipero Serra wrote back to Spain of his discoveries in California, he described the native wild roses, "In the various arroyos along the road and in the place where we are now, besides the wild grape vines, there are Roses of Castile." But *Rosa californica* with its single, five-petaled, pink flowers, more closely resembles the form and blooms of *Rosa canina*, the dog rose, which had been cultivated for centuries in Europe as a medicinal. Whatever rose the padres thought *Rosa californica* actually was, they no doubt found comfort in finding a familiar vestige of the Old World in their new wilderness.

During this period, the rose was a medicinal of high esteem, used in over thirty-two different remedies. For those who have not seen these old species, they are vastly different from the hybrid teas of today. Some plants are literally sticky to the touch, with fragrant oil exuding from stems and leaves, as well as from the flowers. This oil, thought to contain great curative powers, was often made into an ointment called *unguento rosado* to treat every ill imaginable.

Many of the plants grown at the missions were introduced to California through the Manila galleons. It would seem that with a long sea voyage, the ships would supply the missions only with the most essential commodities, such as foodstuffs and plants that bore crops. Yet the damask rose was among them, for it was not considered ornamental, but an important component of the apothecary of that era. The imported cuttings were rooted and then propagated so there would be roses at every mission and presidio along the way. Of course, the roses also landed at the ranchos; as in *Ramona*, and Gertrude Atherton's love story, the verandas were draped in the luscious flowers, which scented the air and created such a romantic picture of early California.

It is believed that over time other roses then known in Spain were also shipped to the New World. During the sixteenth and seventeenth centuries, roses cultivated were for the most part the same species first discovered by the Romans in various parts of their empire. Many hailed from the Middle East and Asia Minor, as with the damask, which attests to its adaptability to the arid climate and low rainfall of California.

The Romans were sophisticated farmers, and their diet relied heavily on fruits and vegetables, but after the fall of the empire, cultivation of crops in Europe was limited. The only plants to survive these dark ages were those thought to have food or medicinal value, and among them were roses. The monasteries protected them within their orderly walled gardens. European Catholic priests, who were responsible for the preservation of the rose, founded the California missions, so it stands to reason they would consider it a highly valuable plant.

The musk rose, *Rosa moschata*, frequently mentioned in *Ramona*, was also grown in early California, and its unique fragrance is likened to that of beeswax and honey. The seeds from its bright red hips have been found in adobe bricks of the missions. It is thought to have first reached Spain not through the Romans but with the Moors, who occupied much of the Iberian Peninsula. Since these Arab horsemen came from a desert climate, this rose was durable and quick to naturalize in Spain, then later in California.

Old species roses were so important to early Californians because the red and white blooms were the emblem of the Virgin Mary. With a culture dominated by the Catholic church, and with missions central to virtually every settlement, it is understandable that any symbol of saints and God was highly revered. On a different note, potent rose fragrance was capable of overwhelming some of the less attractive odors of human habitation in a warm climate.

Up until recently these roses, cast off for the modern hybrid teas, were nearly impossible to buy. But with a new appreciation of the ability of ancient roses to withstand conditions less than ideal, the old species have been resurrected for our modern version of the dryland mission garden. Musk and damask roses are available from a number of mail-order sources. Be aware that species roses are in fact wild plants and tend to grow into very large brambles if not kept pruned. They flower but once a year over a long period, although the musk rose may become somewhat remontant in very warm parts of southern California. Give them plenty of space, or train them to an arbor or veranda, as did the Spanish.

California Peppertree
Schinus molle

If a single tree could represent the mission era of California, it would be the California peppertree. In front of the Leonis Adobe, lining what was then El Camino Real, stands a windrow of ancient peppers, still thriving well over a hundred years in the dry soil of Los Angeles County. The streets of the rural community where I lived were also planted with peppers, which had grown so large their canopies met over the roadway to create a long tunnel of graceful foliage. After just a few years of periodic irrigation, the trees had become established and thrived on their own despite the lack of water. The peppertree is an excellent candidate for street tree programs in rural or suburban communities suffering from acute lack of shading and a shortage of water.

The thick trunks of older trees on land grants and mission sites,

$\mathcal{V}$ery old peppertrees at the site of the San Diego de Alcala mission before restoration. Note the dissolved remnants of adobe brick buildings in the foreground. (*California State Library*)

with their twisted branches rising skyward, support a bright, lime green canopy of feather-soft foliage. The compound leaves hang loosely pendulous, like tresses of hair, and when fingers of coastal breeze move inland to cool the afternoons, the peppertrees sway in time to a silent Mexican lullaby of long ago. Often maligned as messy and invasive, this tree should be accommodated, not only for its beauty, but its great historical significance as well.

The story of the first peppertree in California places it at Mission San Luis Rey. The tale begins in 1830 in Lima, Peru, with a group of sailors returning to their moored ship. One man reached up into the foliage of the trees shading the street, stripped off some bright red seeds from a dangling cluster, and dropped them into his pocket. He reboarded his ship, which sailed northward to trade in Alta California and dropped anchor at what is now the town of Oceanside.

There the sailor went ashore to visit with the mission padres. At their evening meal, the padres and guests discussed which Peruvian plants might grow well in the California climate. The sailor remembered his pocketful of pepper seeds and offered them to a priest.

Having no idea what the seed would produce, the padre set them aside and promptly forgot about them.

Not until two years later were the seeds rediscovered and planted in a row out in front of the mission. Treated poorly by livestock and vaqueros, only one peppertree seedling survived, but from this single individual came the thousands of trees distributed among the missions, pueblos, presidios, and ranchos of early California. It should be noted, however, that two peppertrees of opposite sexes are required to produce viable seed, but perhaps a dying male tree had managed to pollinate one or more crops of seeds before it succumbed.

One disease that indirectly yet strongly afflicted these trees was black scale. The scale is not necessarily damaging to the peppertree itself, but to citrus growing nearby. Tragically, the threat of black scale to southern California citrus groves in the 1920s sent farmers into a panic. They promptly felled and burned any peppers in the vicinity of their groves and thereby destroyed many of the oldest and most magnificent specimens.

California peppertrees have great landscape value. They are equally at home at the Hotel Bel Air as they are in the Mohave Desert. Not particularly fast-growing, the round-headed trees are bushy but can be thinned to reveal the attractive branching structure. Just as with eucalyptus, few plants will grow close to the trunk of a peppertree; it is believed that peppertrees exude a chemical to discourage competition. Strongly rooted, they will hunt for water over a large area, which is the means by which they did so well at the missions, but modern root control devices can reduce this bad habit. Leaves are compound, made up of small leaflets. These leaves can be a problem in swimming pools. Trees require both male and female to produce peppercorns, which occur only on female trees. The red outer, paper-thin shells fall away easily, and the hard seeds can be painful for bare feet on paved surfaces. Despite these habits, the pepper is still a wonderful tree for California and should be given due respect.

Date Palms
Phoenix dactylifera

Date palms are grown commercially in California only in the southeastern deserts, where summer temperatures are hot enough to ripen the fruit. An old saying, "Palms must have their roots in the water and the head in fire," explains that the abundant water supply

Many of the date palms planted at the missions survived into the twentieth century. These mature specimens at the San Diego de Alcala mission are considered as old as the mission itself. Beside them is a good example of the kind of *huerta* or walled garden, grown at the missions. Remnants of once larger adobe walls, which have dissolved after losing their tile caps, attest to the character of the early gardens and their enclosures. (*California State Library*)

beneath Palm Springs and nearby communities is a second reason why the date groves produce so well there. Early expeditions were supplied with all sorts of dried foods from Mexico, including dates descended from the groves in North Africa. The seeds from these dates were usually planted, developing into large, broad-headed trees. Although these did not provide fruit, the padres valued their foliage for processions on Palm Sunday, and the long feather-shaped fronds were ideal for thatch roofs and fencing. The trees were also highly drought-tolerant, growing with little to no care.

Phoenix dactylifera is closely related to the popular landscape palm *Phoenix canariensis*, the Canary Island palm. However, the Canary Island palm does not produce edible dates. Although there are references to the padres growing the Canary Island palm, this does not seem logical. Why would they ship seeds or even potted plants of an inedible palm from a West African island halfway around the world to plant at the missions? It stands to reason that the true date palm was the only species on mission grounds.

Old photographs of missions at the turn of the century frequently show very old date palms, which managed to survive abandonment after the demise of the mission system. One palm at Mission San Diego was thought to be 180 years old when it finally died. While cutting up the massive trunk, a large number of American bullets dated to 1850 were clustered at about "man" height. It is strange that this palm, first planted for its symbolism in a religious ritual, should have become a place of execution. The condemned would have been tied to the trunk, then shot by a firing squad, hence the lead.

The date palm does not make a good landscape palm for our gardens. The Canary Island palm is similar in size and shape, but its fronds are more lush and attractive. Its trunk is also a bit cleaner, whereas date palm fronds break off unevenly and are more densely spaced on the trunk. Date palms can become immense and are there-

Commercially grown date palms in the inland deserts of California, where they fruit prolifically. (*Stellman Collections, California State Library*)

A cactus hedge photographed in 1886 at the San Gabriel mission. It was planted by Padre Zabridos to protect the garden and vineyard from roaming bands of horses and Indians. (*California History Society, Title Insurance and Trust Photo Collection, Department of Special Collections, University of Southern California Library*)

fore not recommended for urban or even suburban residential gardens. But for those who live in communities in and around the Mohave and Colorado deserts, date palms can be considered home orchard trees. As street trees throughout California, the Canary Island palm has proven to be stately, and old plantings appear today more as monuments to our climate than just another row of ubiquitous palm trees.

Prickly Pear Cactus
Opuntia spp.

Of all the cacti native to the southwestern United States, the prickly pear is the most easily identified. Another common name is beaver tail, because its flat, paddle-shaped growths are similar to the shape of the animal's tail. *Opuntia* is native to parts of southern

California, and an enormous number of species range from South America to as far north as Montana, proving the wide variation in resistance to winter cold. In Mexico the plant is called *nopal* and was used by the Aztecs long before the Spanish Conquest. *Opuntia* is such a large genus that it includes the cigar-shaped chollas and deceivingly fuzzy "teddy bear" cactus, both quite different in appearance from the prickly pear.

Perhaps the most curious species is *Opuntia cochenillifera*, a type of prickly pear commonly called cochineal for the red dye of that name harvested from it. Since prehistoric times the native peoples of Central and South America produced a bright red dye—the Spaniards discovered its use among the Aztecs. It was particularly valuable as a textile dye because of its natural permanence, but improved modern dyes have virtually eliminated commercial demand for cochineal. Compared to dyes available in Europe at the time, cochineal was superior, and Cortez was ordered to send as much as he could back to Spain, where it became precious and was used to pay tribute to the Spanish crown. The industry of cochineal manufacture then spread from the Iberian Peninsula to India, Algiers, and South Africa, all countries with very hot climates and limited water supply. The forgiving prickly pear was no doubt a sturdy and welcome agricultural crop.

It was believed the dye was a vegetable product of the cochineal cactus itself, due to the coloring that covered the surface of each paddle. But in 1703, when early microscopes came into use, it was discovered that the red coloring was not a part of the plant, but in fact a tiny insect related to our common garden scale. So the cochineal *Opuntia* propagators early on inadvertently transported the insects on each cutting, and clean plants were automatically contaminated by others growing nearby. After discovery of the tiny organism, growers placed cochineal insects at the joints of each leaf, where they reproduced very quickly into sizeable populations. Every four months or so, most of the insects were collected by brushing them off into a container, then spread out to dry in the sun. The dye was produced by pulverizing the insects into a powder, and it is reported that over seventy thousand of them are required to produce just one pound of dye.

In 1787 Captain Arthur Phillip shipped cochineal and other species of *Opuntia* to dry Australia, where he planned to develop a dye plantation. This was a dangerous move because whenever a resilient exotic plant is introduced to a new ecosystem, there is the chance that its vigor will overwhelm the native species that are criti-cal to wildlife. From this initial contamination, prickly pear escaped, and by 1925 (less than 150 years) twenty different species of the spiny weed had literally choked off 60 million acres. Concerned for the loss of grazing and forage, the Commonwealth Prickly Pear Board was established to find some means of control. Entomologists (insect sci-entists) discovered that a moth from Argentina, aptly named *Cactoblastis cactorum*, fed upon *Opuntia* species. Large numbers of them were imported, then released in the most infested prickly pear areas. Within seven years the moth had wiped out all the *Opuntia* cacti, and Australia reclaimed her ravaged countryside.

Prickly pear, a highly versatile plant, was used many different ways in old California. At the missions in the nearly treeless coastal plain of southern California, it became an important material for fencing. The cactus roots easily: One simply breaks off a paddle and pushes it partway into the soil. In fact, detached paddles are known to retain their viability for almost two years. With this ease of propaga-tion, fences of sharp, spiny plants could be planted quickly, and rela-tively fast growth made them formidable barriers in a short time.

Just about every part of the most common variety, *Opuntia ficus-indica*, is edible. Proof of this can be found in the supermarket, where its flat paddles, called *nopales* are sold with spines already removed. It is cooked and stewed in Mexican soups. The missions often suffered from periodic drought; during these times the shortage of food forced the padres to use prickly pear leaves with the thorns removed as alternative livestock fodder. In addition, the sticky juice of nopales that had been boiled and crushed was added to mortar and whitewash to make them more tacky and stick better to adobe walls of early ranch and mission buildings.

The fruit of the prickly pear cactus, by far its best feature, is called *tunas* in Mexico. The *tunas* are the fleshy seed capsules that follow the brightly colored flowers blooming at the tips of the leaves. A ripe *tuna* can be similar in size to a baseball, but oval in shape. Its skin is tough and heavily spiked, but removal of the thorns and peeling yields a suc-culent flesh much like that of a melon, but with small seeds scattered throughout. In old California the *tunas* were often dried, or cooked into a sweet syrup, as sugar was not commonly available.

On the ranchos, the prickly pear was a source of soft wood. Some of the plants would reach treelike proportions, with trunks two to three feet thick. The center of the trunks became woody, far

$\mathcal{L}$uther Burbank's spineless prickly pear cactus, heavily laden with fruit in the fertile, moist soil of Santa Rosa, California. (*California State Library*)

stronger than the surrounding flesh. In Mexico and no doubt early California, very old plants were cut down while still living, then left outdoors in the shade to dry for many months, dehydrating slowly without cracking.

The vaqueros of that time valued *Opuntia* wood because it could be handcarved and then fitted with a covering of tooled leather. It is believed the very broad, flat saddle horn of the Mexican saddle and its heavy pommel was developed to make these soft opuntia wood saddle trees stronger. Upon this flat surface the vaquero is said to have attached a disk of silver that he could shine to a mirrorlike reflective sheen, supposedly to admire himself while riding the range.

The prickly pear fruit was widely used by Native Americans of our southwest deserts, particularly the Apache, who have legends regarding its spiny nature. They cooked fresh fruit into a sweet sauce that is again becoming popular in traditional Southwestern cuisine. The Indians often dried the *tunas* for storage and sometimes fermented the juice into a stimulating prickly pear wine.

Luther Burbank, the famous California plant breeder, realized the potential of this cactus as an agricultural crop. The only problems were that the vicious spines were dangerous to livestock and they had to be removed before the flesh was rendered for any type of product. Without them, livestock could freely browse upon the leaves, and collection of the fruit would be much easier. Burbank's intent was to create a plant that could transform the dry deserts of the West into productive farmland.

After extensive experimentation, he produced a spineless cactus, but the Department of Agriculture called his strain a hoax and suggested the spines had been chewed off by desert rodents or other grazing animals. The experts also asserted that for the cactus to grow rapidly enough for a bona fide crop, it would require nearly as much water as more versatile alfalfa. Two things put a stop to Burbank's work with the cactus. First, he was denied renewal of the Carnegie grant that funded his research, and it was determined that prickly pear cactus simply did not contain sufficient nutrients to support livestock.

Prickly pear makes a good Southwestern garden plant, especially where water supplies are limited. It flowers profusely, with daisies of brilliant yellow, red, or orange petals that draw hummingbirds and bees. Beware of planting it near activity areas, since the spines are unforgiving and may cause serious injuries. Tongs or heavy gloves are necessary just to pick the *tunas*, but imagine what it would take to eradicate a dense stand of the stuff. And since the leaves can remain viable for years, they can root just about anywhere they are discarded. It's a good idea to prune your prickly pears on a regular basis to keep them controlled.

The *tunas* of prickly pear cactus are ripe when they turn scarlet red. Wear thick gloves and use tongs to pick them. First break or cut off all the large spines. Use steel wool to rub away all the fine, hairlike fiber tufts at the base of each spine; these fibers are very sharp and can be a painful nuisance. Then skin the fruit as you would a tomato or peach by simply dropping it into a pot of boiling water for a minute or so, then plunge it into cold water. The skin should slide off easily.

There are many other species of *Opuntia*, which grow in varying forms. Cholla, one of the more well known, consists of fat, cigar-shaped segments, which are viciously spined. Some call these "jumping chollas" because the spines come out so easily, they seem to leap at their victims brushing by the plant. The cholla thorns are also lined with microscopic barbs, which make extracting them from human skin very difficult and painful.

The Mickey Mouse *Opuntia* is a smaller plant and lacks the big spines of the other species. It is protected by clusters of fine, velvety, hairlike spines that are nearly microscopic. Their softness invites touch, but the filaments will remain in the skin and are too small to pick out. Children are often the prey of this seemingly benign succulent.

Fruits of the Missions

Before the missions in California were established, there was a similar chain of fifteen mission outposts in what is now northern Mexico. These were founded by the Jesuits, who were not as inclined to agriculture as the Franciscans, who entered the scene in 1768. In the first expedition of Fra Junipero Serra to what is now San Diego, the King of Spain was represented by Don Jose de Galvez, who ordered the carrying of seed for fruit, vegetables, and flowering plants. From his foresight, the garden of San Diego was established, and from it sprung the beginnings of California agriculture.

The lemon was introduced into Spain by the Moors sometime in the twelfth century, and Crusaders were also reported to have brought seeds of lemons, limes, and oranges home with them from the Holy Land. The seed was distributed throughout Mexico and Central America by Spanish colonials. Two centuries later citrus trees, by now well established in Latin America, were brought to California with the Franciscans and planted at the missions. Citrus was also considered a medicinal plant, with essential oils added to a variety of preparations. The custom of eating lemon with fish ensured that if a fish bone were to be accidently swallowed, the juice of the lemon would help the stomach digest it.

Scurvy, a disease caused by vitamin C deficiency, plagued people denied fresh fruits, greens, or vegetables in sufficient quantities. It was common among men isolated on board ship, loosening teeth, causing anemia, and bringing a host of other unsavory symptoms. In fact, scurvy claimed the lives of 160 men on Vasco da Gama's 1497 voyage around the Cape of Good Hope to India. The padres at remote missions suffered from scurvy, which was later widespread in the goldfields. Citrus was eventually recognized as the best preventative of this killer, making it a necessity in New World settlements, not just a flavorful food or minor medicinal.

As mentioned before, the mission grounds were dusty, dry places, and not at all similar to our modern image of a garden. But in the treeless deserts of the south coast, the greenery and shade of mission orchards and palms must have seemed much like Eden. George Vancouver, a British explorer of the Pacific coast, visited missions during his journey. He describes the Mission Santa Clara in 1792 as containing a fine orchard of pears, apples, plums, figs, oranges, grapes, peaches, and pomegranates.

Unfortunately, after secularization of the missions, these fruit trees were the first to suffer. Only the olives, pears, pomegranates, and occasional grapevines survived, due to their origins in dry Mediterranean regions. However, the mission decline did not occur overnight, but was gradual, spanning many years. Just as the sites were robbed of their building materials, early settlers also transplanted or propagated the proven mission varieties for planting at their own farms. One of these was the mission olive, so labeled in 1880 because it originated at these sites; it became the primary California variety. The others, especially pears and grapes, became the scion stock for California's first commercial orchards.

William Brewer describes the grapevines of early California in his journal during travels for the United States Geological Survey. While mapping portions of Santa Barbara, he encountered an enormous and highly prolific plant of great age at Montecito, where it literally overwhelmed the garden of José Dominguez. Brewer measured the trunk and proclaimed it over thirty inches in circumference, with the branches radiating out to cover about four thousand square feet. The yield was estimated at three to four tons of grapes per year, with bunches weighing up to seven pounds each. This vine was said to have been a cutting from vines at San Antonio Mission in Monterey County, and was planted before 1800. Brewer's enthusiastic reports of this immense vine reflect the surprise of most Easterners upon discovering that the California climate supports immense harvests unheard of elsewhere in the United States.

Flowers of the Missions for Altar and Medicine

During a time when plants were watered with a bucket and a dipper gourd, growing flowers simply to beautify outdoor spaces was considered wasteful. In a country of frequent drought and a very long growing season, the allocation of part of a scant water supply for purely aesthetic purposes was unreasonable. But the Franciscans were Catholic priests, and their lives revolved around the calendar of the old church—with feast days when processions and high mass called for appropriate decoration. In this sense, the flowers became a crop for ritual and were cultivated as a sign of faith and adoration.

The Catholic orders of the Old World have a long history of medicine and agriculture. Monks, skilled as botanical apothecaries, cultivated *materia medica* with close attention. The Franciscans no doubt learned their knowledge of medicine through monastery gardens, and in the faraway missions of the New World, it was essential that medicinal plants be cultivated. We know the padres grew *dormidera*—the annual *Papaver somniferum*, or opium poppy. Not only did it provide a pain-relieving substance, the copious seed was also used in cooking. A native of the Santa Barbara Islands, *Solidago californica* was discovered through the Indians as a tea for fevers. These and many European medicinal herbs appeared in the mission physic gardens and may have been mistaken by some as strictly ornamental plants.

Of all the Catholic celebrations at the missions, the processions of Palm Sunday must have been the most memorable. The long, feather fronds of the date palm can easily reach ten feet in length; the neophytes (as do modern-day Catholics) carried them into the church for mass on that Sunday before Easter. Calla lilies were favored for Easter as a symbol of the Resurrection. All white lilies, as grown in Europe, were regarded as emblems of purity and beauty, devoted to the Madonna. To commemorate the journey of Mary to her cousin Elizabeth, a vase of three white lilies would be placed beside the statue of the Virgin. This tradition originated from a tale about three white lilies that magically appeared on a monastery altar. Their presence is said to confirm the faith of a questionable abbot who presided over an order of Dominican monks.

The marigold, or possibly the calendula, was no doubt present in the mission gardens because it also symbolizes the Virgin Mary. The old species were simple daisies, and the petals were the "rays of glory" often depicted around the head of Mary in religious paintings. Calendula petals are likely to have doubled as a medicinal because in eighteenth- and nineteenth-century Europe, as well as in the United States, they were used to pack wounds and stanch the flow of blood. Hollyhocks, or "holy-hocks," were important flowers as they were brought back to Europe from the Holy Land by the Crusaders. Consecrated as the "Flor de San Jose," they decorated the church with their tall spires when St. Joseph was honored on his feast day.

One of the most notable flowers of mystical symbolism is the passionflower, now a common vine in our California landscapes. Early Spanish botanical drawings by eighteenth-century explorers indicates it was first discovered in South America during the mission era and was even transported to Spain for cultivation. This lends credence to the legends that the great stories of its Christian symbolism, based on the complex architecture of the blooms and its other parts was begun in New World missions, where the vine was also planted. Imagine how this single plant, with its unique beauty, could be used to illustrate the basics of Christianity to the Indians. As a vine, even its growth was allegorically like the spiritual growth of the neophyte, or new Catholic, who requires support, notably that of the Lord's strength.

Every part of the passionflower's exotic and intricate bloom was importantly related to aspects of the Crucifixion. (And even as an unopened bud it represents the star the three wise men saw in the East.) The flower's ten petals suggest ten Apostles, excluding Judas for his betrayal and Peter for his denial. Christ's loneliness is seen in that the flowers grow singly on each stem.

The vine's tendrils, with which it clings for support, symbolize the whips of the scourging. The bloom's purple coloring is like that of the robe placed on Jesus' shoulders during his mockery, and the corolla is the crown of thorns (or a halo). The central receptacle is the pillar of the cross; the five anthers are the hammers of the Crucifixion (one to attach the cross' horizontal beam; two to nail Jesus' hands to the cross, and one for his feet; and one to nail the charge "The King of the Jews" over his head); and the flower's three stigmas are the nails that pierced Jesus' flesh. The small seed vessel represents the sponge filled with vinegar. Last, the five red spots on each of the passionflower's leaves are symbolic of the slain Christ's five wounds: the four nail holes and the spear wound made in his side to verify his death.

DETAILS: ADOBE AND ROSES

Gardens designed to complement Spanish- or Mediterranean-style architecture may depend on these plants of the Old West, but they also require construction materials for paving and enclosure. How materials are combined and arranged helps enhance outdoor spaces and make these spaces evoke the original missions or ranchos.

Fountains

In hot and dry countries with Mediterranean climates, water is a precious resource. In the old days every household needed it around the home, for livestock, and to support plants. If there was a single architectural element most characteristic of the Spanish era in California, it would be the fountain. Every mission had its own irrigation system, which fed one or more fountains. The original fountains were rather plain, but over the years they have become quite decorative and use far more glazed ceramic tile.

Tiles

The greatest mission contribution during this time was the veranda, which later evolved into what we call a patio. Due to the lack of wood in southern California, the veranda was typically paved with terra-cotta clay tiles. Those we call Saltillo pavers are very similar to the ones made by the neophytes, which were molded by hand and sun-dried complete with footprints of cats and birds, which had walked across the field of still-damp clay tiles. At old mission sites the tiles themselves have eroded into shallow depressions, while the mortar joints still stand up stiffly. This illustrates the problem with Mexican tiles for outdoor use, a problem compounded by a tendency to warp and subsequently crack. The tiles simply do not hold up, even with a sealer. Higher quality, dense terra-cotta pavers from Italy, and some from the United States resist this erosion but are considerably more expensive. But their even sizes and consistent flatness greatly reduce breakage, and they are less labor-intensive to install.

Although probably there were few, if any, glazed ceramic tiles at the missions, they did play a vital role in both Spain and later Mexico. This is yet another component of the Islamic architectural influence left in Spain by the Moors. The aesthetic necessity of tiles must be viewed through the eyes of a North African, who would have very few decorative plants at his disposal, and even less water to grow them with. Natural color would therefore be lacking in the household courtyards, so the brilliant, unfading hues of glazed ceramic tiles offered beauty and interest all year. The tiles were incorporated with terra-cotta pavers into floor patterns and to face risers on steps. Tile patterns were worked into masonry walls, the seats of permanent benches, and of course became critical features of the fountains.

Glazed ceramic tiles for today's Western gardens should be carefully selected, particularly in areas in the north where winters can be quite frosty. Glazed tile is made with clay of varying porosity. Saltillo pavers are porous beneath their glazed surface and will tend to absorb water. If that water freezes, it will expand and force the tiles out of place. Many Mexican patterned tiles are made for interior use or for outdoors use only in frost-free climates. "Frostproof" tiles are more dense and resist absorption of water. A simple but not infallible test for porosity is to turn a tile facedown and place a few drops of water on the back. If the water soaks in, chances are it is not suitable for outdoor use. However, on a good frostproof tile, like those used for swimming pools, the test drops of water will bead up and remain on the back surface indefinitely.

Walls

The hallmark of a Spanish-inspired garden is the use of adobe brick made from naturally occurring deposits of heavy clay. The bricks used at mission sites and various ranchos throughout much of the state were actually quite large, measuring about one foot wide and two feet long. The clay was mixed with bits of manure and straw, packed into a mold, then set out to dry in the hot sun. One of the disadvantages of using adobe as a building material is that it cannot be easily reinforced with steel. To build the great heights of the mission churches, the walls had to be nearly five feet thick at the base, gradually tapering as they grew taller.

Another factor governing the viability of adobe is erosion by water. Adobe bricks are sun-dried, not fired, and thus have practically no resistance to rain or water from other sources. Walls must be capped with tile or other impervious materials to discourage rain erosion, typically with roof tile or terra-cotta floor tiles. But the side walls are still vulnerable, which is why most adobe structures of the wealthy were coated with a thick plaster made of oyster shell. It is suggested that the warm pinks of Mexican plasters were obtained by incorporating animal blood into the mixture.

For most gardens true adobe is not a practical option, but there are other materials that simulate the visual same effect. The most valuable material is called slump block, a concrete-based masonry unit that was removed from its mold ahead of time so its outer walls would bow outward. The units can be purchased in many different sizes, depending on the height and width of the proposed wall. Because each block has empty central cells, they function just like any other concrete block and can be heavily reinforced.

Slump block walls may be capped with concrete, but this does little to enhance the character. To remain in keeping with the padres' adobe walls, terra-cotta floor tiles or red bricks make a durable, easily constructed cap. Slump blocks come in various earth tones, or they can be painted to suggest plaster but still reveal the textured surface of each unit.

Masonry walls of any sort are expensive to build but ensure a long-lasting, secure enclosure. Building codes vary, but most restrict height to no more than six feet. Lower seat walls may serve different purposes, such as defining spaces within the garden and retaining soil for raised planters, while offering the amenity of permanent outdoor seating. Seat walls are usually eighteen to twenty-four inches high and at least twelve inches wide, making sitting on them comfortable. The caps of low seat walls are far more visible and may utilize colorful glazed tile caps to provide a smooth, clean surface. Terra-cotta and red brick are also suitable caps.

Fences

The *huertas*, or courtyards, of early California required fencing to protect plants from livestock and wildlife. In modern gardens and homesites, there can be the need to enclose livestock, and the rustic designs of woven paling fences are a labor-intensive but highly attractive solution. If lodgepole pine or other types of "sticks" are available, paling is a viable method of fence building, but for the most part it is prohibitively expensive except in small quantities.

Living fences act much like a hedge in the dryland garden. The two most common species are the prickly pear cactus and the century plant (*Agave americana*). Although they may not actually surround a garden or livestock, their linear planting can create a powerful statement. If propagated at home and planted with patience, they will over many years develop into a significant garden element. Their formidable spines make these plants a serious barrier. For example, a yard enclosed with prickly pear assures you that no one will ever "climb the back fence" to trespass onto the property. These hedges can also line driveways or create a visual barrier as well. And with its bright flowers and delicious fruit, prickly pear should probably be considered a part of the home orchard.

Pots

For small city gardens throughout California, gardening in pots may be the only means of adding greenery and color to a patio or a courtyard. As mentioned in the opening of this chapter, people in desert climates found that potted plants can be made to survive on discarded "gray water" from the household. In today's container gardens, useful gray water might be that of the bathtub or washing machine—any water that is unlikely to contain grease or other undesirable byproducts. In fact, many detergents contain high quantities of nitrates and phosphates, which are two of the three major nutrients needed by plants. Laundry water using detergents free of perfumes, dyes, and other additives proves quite compatible with landscape plants as long as it is not overused. In many gardens this may serve as the critical emergency water source to save landscape plants during rationing or drought.

Terra-cotta clay pots are the most characteristic of container gardens, but today there are also good look-alike pots made of light-resistant plastics. True terra-cotta pots have a few drawbacks. First, they are heavy, and if the pots must be moved around with the seasons, they can be difficult to handle. They are fragile and easily broken, particularly large pots containing very heavy plants. Moisture loss through porous clay is much faster than with a plastic pot, so terra-cotta is less thrifty for drought-conscious gardening. As the water moves through the clay, it tends to leave behind a white mineral deposit on the outside of the pot. This is why the clay discolors so badly where there is a large amount of salt or other minerals in the water supply. However, it can be removed with special acids and lots of elbow grease.

The plastic look-alikes are light enough when empty to be

picked up and easily moved around. They do not discolor, and they retain moisture in the soil far longer. Yet plastic also has its problems. There are now many different manufacturers, which makes product quality and longevity variable. Thinner walls may break, and certain types of plastic can become brittle through long-term exposure to ultraviolet sunlight. These weaknesses may be compounded by extremes of heat and cold. Some of the better companies which supply architects make good products which are durable and last a long time. These will be quite a bit more expensive than the cheaper models you may find at discount home-improvement stores.

Pots may be planted with any type of plant that remains in scale with the container. Use them to place vines at the bases of posts or along walls, or plant with small palms to provide soft foliage backgrounds to color pots. Try wide bowls with upright cactus or hanging pots of cascading succulents—either is uniquely Spanish. Small trees, such as citrus and oleander standards, in large pots allow instant shading, fragrance, and color. The most popular fillers are annual bedding plants, which may be changed with the seasons into new and exciting color combinations.

PICKET FENCES AND ORCHARDS

*B*y 1840 the great westward migration was practically over everywhere but in the territories of California and Oregon. Free land was no longer available in the prime agricultural states of the Midwest. Yet American pioneers of the prairie were still eager to move on and could not resist the glowing accounts of an almost mystical California. It is estimated that in 1840 there were only about 380 Americans in California, the balance of the residents being a mixture of Spanish, Mexicans, and Native Americans. Letters and diaries of migratory settlers viewed these residents as uneducated, lazy, and unable to use the fertile land and mild climate for anything more productive than far-flung, relaxed cattle ranches.

Prior to statehood there was very little contact between California and the East because overland trails through the mighty Sierra were few and treacherous. Most of these were discovered by beaver trappers who had worked out their previous locations and were forced to follow the beaver westward. The journey for the first immigrants reaching California overland was long and dangerous, their goal not to settle in a new part of the United States but in a separate country governed by Mexico. A handful of early, enterprising souls who first realized the agricultural potential of the state managed to brave the long journey through Fort Bridger and the Humboldt

Sink, and finally to climb the Sierra Nevada to a pass that is now Immigrant Gap.

A second route, part of the Santa Fe Trail, passed below the south end of the Sierra, then over the Tehachapi Mountains into San Gabriel and the Los Angeles basin. But this was a dry trip, passing mostly through the parched southwestern deserts, which extended almost to the coast. This forbidding landscape explains why the majority of farmer immigrants concentrated in the north end of the state, where rainfall and rivers were more plentiful.

There are numerous fertile valleys within the coastal ranges, but the greatest opportunities for settlement lay in the great Sacramento-San Joaquin Central Valley, with its deep, fertile soils. The many rivers draining the western slopes of the Sierra passed through the valley, providing copious amounts of water throughout the dry summer months. The plains along the river courses were incredibly rich, built up over a countless millennia of flooding. Today these are some of our most productive farmlands.

But early farmers saw the valley far differently. It was widely believed that the valley soil that supported vast grasslands had few trees because it was sterile ground. Yet years later these same farmers rejoiced over land that would support two crops within one growing season, a feat unheard of in the East and Midwest. The valley lowlands were poorly drained and literally packed with tules, reeds, and all sorts of dense, marshy growth. As the insect populations were horrendous in the summer, Native Americans resided there only during the winter, returning for the annual migration of waterfowl flocks so dense "the sky grew dark with their passing."

Yet the land was a perpetual trial of fire and water. Seas of tule often caught fire, and the flames ripped through the valley at incredible speed, consuming years of accumulated dead vegetation. One old valley resident's grandfather had seen these great fires, which he claimed moved faster than a man could run and often caused terrible disasters. The smoke from wildfires clouded the valley and fouled its air for weeks on end. Flooding was also commonplace, with the fickle Sierra Nevada weather suddenly sending enormous amounts of water into the valley. In 1862 record floodwaters stood in the Sacramento Valley from the foothills of the Sierra to the Coast Ranges, with only the Sutter Buttes standing dry in its midst. William Brewer, in his book *Up and Down California*, describes the disaster in detail. Rainfall figures state that over one hundred inches of rain fell in the Sierra foothills, and not until the following August were roads through the valley passable.

The early farmers no doubt paid dearly to gain their fertile soil. Slowly, at almost a trickle, the first wagons passed over the mountains. To do so above Donner Lake, the travelers would have to disassemble their wagons and hoist each piece over the summits. This was made even more difficult as the Sierra Nevada was the last and most brutal range to be surmounted after a very long trail westward.

Perhaps the most famous early pioneers were those of the Donner party, who in 1846 set out for California from the Midwest. Their first error was in starting out too late in the spring. In an attempt to make up for their tardiness and reach the Sierra earlier, they followed Lansford Hastings, who claimed to have found an alternate route that might save as much time as a week. Unfortunately, Hastings was unclear about the route, and the already stressed Donner wagon train found the shortcut not only more rugged but a longer distance than the main trail. By the time the ragged Donner wagons reached what was then Truckee Lake, an early winter set in. By the end of November, there was ten feet of snow on the ground, forcing the party to dig in and wait until spring before attempting to cross the higher peaks. Part of the wagon train was camped north of what is now the town of Truckee at Alder Creek. Proof of the depth of the snow can still be seen in the state park at what is now Donner Lake, where tree stumps as tall as twenty feet show where the travelers had stood to cut the trees down for firewood.

Already short on provisions, those at Alder Creek and others at Donner Lake eventually starved to death. Relief efforts at Sutter's Fort were hindered by the Mexican War, which had garnered most of the able-bodied men. Only months later when the war subsided did relief parties manage to reach the high country. And there it was discovered that to survive, many of the living had resorted to consuming their dead.

For the remainder of the nineteenth century, this story of disaster would be told and retold around countless immigrant camps, a grisly reminder of how crucial timing was to passing safely through the unforgiving Sierra Nevada. Yet this did not stop the families of farmers lured by tales of California's vast, fertile land and mild climate.

Two important events occurred during the last part of the 1840s that were important to the future of California farmers. First, the land became a territory of the United States in 1848, then was granted statehood two years later. But perhaps more important was the discovery of placer gold at Sutter's Mill in Coloma.

With the privileges of statehood, the residents of California began to challenge the ownership of land. Many of the enormous land grants and mission sites were finally lost by their original owners and soon became occupied by new settlers. The early immigrants of the 1840s had the first opportunity to settle the best land, and this placed them in an excellent position to capitalize on the impending Gold Rush. It cannot be stressed enough that the real wealth of this period was not necessarily made in the mines, but rather in satisfying the high demand for goods, namely foodstuffs, which exacted exorbitant prices. The freight and mercantile trades were two other similarly lucrative areas of enterprise.

The Gold Rush also pushed the population of Anglos in the state from 380 in 1840 to an incredible 225,000 in 1852. Eighty percent of the growth was between 1848 and 1852. The pre-Gold Rush settlers were already homesteaded or set up in business, so later arrivals lured by promises of wealth could not all be successful. A vast majority of miners were left disillusioned and destitute in California, often turning their hands to the same trades they once plied in the East and Midwest. This resulted in the appearance of a new class of opportunists during the 1850s, many of whom became farmers, as the state offered such an ideal climate.

Others turned to ranching, as did Henry Miller, and his gentle art of accumulating land grants from financially destitute Mexicans left him with a massive portion of the San Joaquin Valley and the surrounding foothills. Far wiser than most, he drained and irrigated, built levees, and planted his bottomland with silage and other important feed crops that were sold or supplied to his own enormous herds. And his attention to developing ground water sources and reservoirs helped him survive some of California's most devastating droughts, while the ranchers around him who lacked such foresight perished.

The farmers of the 1840s, 1850s, and even later helped shape the face of the state as we know it today. Here was a group who recognized the quality of our lands, whether they be for pastures, orchards, or row crops. The families that built California from their farms and ranches contributed a tremendous amount to our aesthetic, which combines the residual Spanish influence with those of eastern American origins.

The dooryard gardens of our agrarian communities were for the

A homestead in the Sacramento Valley. (*Community Memorial Museum*)

most part the domains of wives and daughters. These women cultivated the essential culinary and medicinal herbs, along with flowers,
while the men were occupied with the commercial aspects of the
farming. Herbs, it must be remembered, were important in an era
lacking refrigeration because their potent oils disguised the taste of
tainted meats.

The women of California's early farmsteads were rugged individuals, and many had weathered long winters on treeless prairies.
Imagine how fertile and lush our land must have appeared in com-
parison. They often arrived overland by wagon, hardened by long and
arduous trips that took the lives of many of their sisters and children.
If the journey was by ship to San Francisco, they would either spend
months sailing around the Horn or take a shorter but more strenu-
ous hike through malaria-infested jungles at the Isthmus of Panama.
Either way, these stalwart souls were often just as isolated as the mission padres, and thus were equally reliant on botanical plants as
essential treatments of illness.

Women leaving their old homes carried seeds, bulbs, and roots
of useful plants. They were as important to them as cooking pots and
sewing needles. It is interesting to note that the wagon routes during
the mid- to late nineteenth century were littered with the possessions
of travelers who found the weight of a cast iron stove or a carved

The Sierra Nevada at 10,000 feet near Mount Whitney.

The Mohave Desert.

A Sierra mountain pass.

Section of oak tree with woodpecker holes, some still containing acorns.

California's oak woodlands.

A palm grove at Agua Caliente outside Palm Springs, showing the barren desert that surrounds the oasis. In such an unforgiving landscape, the palms were essential to life and were preserved by the Cahuilla people who lived there.

Oak tree and wildflowers in the hills. (*California Department of Water Resources*)

$\mathcal{H}$uts similar to this one were built by many California tribes, the materials ranging from palm frond thatch in the desert oases to tule and cattail in the Central Valley.

$\mathcal{A}$ young digger pine, illustrating its lanky form and wispy foliage.

$\mathcal{T}$he mature cones of digger pine.

$\mathcal{T}$he blue-green spikes of a low-growing species of sagebrush in dry mountain terrain.

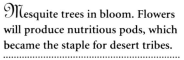

Mesquite trees in bloom. Flowers will produce nutritious pods, which became the staple for desert tribes.

*Y*ucca brevifolia flowers. (*California Department of Water Resources*)

*M*anzanita leaves and flowers.

*Y*ucca brevifolia. (*California Department of Water Resources*)

The varying forms of *Agave americana*, one with the solid blue leaves, and the other variegated.

An agave with its tall bloom stalk.

The thick, blue-gray *Agave americana* leaf, showing the edges serrated with sharp thorns.

An ornamental variety of angel's trumpet with flowers ten inches long.

$\mathcal{D}$ark blue-flowering California lilac.

$\mathcal{T}$he more pale-colored, low-growing *Ceanothus thyrsifolius* of the Sierra Nevada.

$\mathcal{T}$he smoky fall coloring of western redbud, which ranges from yellow to a deep magenta, depending on its location.

These red berries are why California toyon is also known as Christmas berry.

Toyon during the summer, when its evergreen broadleaf foliage is welcome in the dry landscape.

The snow white center of the soaproot bulb was grated to make excellent soap for washing or as a glue to seal baskets. The fibers made stiff brushes.

California poppy.

Bush lupine.

Mission San Gabriel Arcangel in 1832. (*Hubert Lowman*)

The fully restored Mission Santa Barbara was founded 1786.

Mission San Diego de Alcala, built of adobe brick. (*California Department of Water Resources*)

𝒯his pocket garden is part of a central mission courtyard. The large clay olla, which is remarkably preserved, held either water or olive oil.

𝒯he rooms of most adobe homes were connected by this sort of veranda. It became a meeting place, well used and always stocked with benches.

𝒥n many rancho courtyards, nothing but shade trees and vines trained to the veranda were grown.

An old rose variety typical of those at the missions.

White roses on an arch at Mission San Juan Capistrano.

This ancient California peppertree stands in the old city square of Santa Barbara.

The gnarled trunk of the peppertree is most visible when it is mature, and this may be one of the largest specimens in California.

This prickly pear has blue-green paddles with purple highlights.

A prickly pear with long, thin leaves.

The fruit of the prickly pear cactus, the red coloring indicating it is fully ripe and sweet.

During the Spanish period citrus grew under these dry, inhospitable conditions on both mission and rancho.

Olive trees were favored for their fruit and as shade trees. They were the source of an important oil used in lamps and cooking. This olive blends perfectly into the dusty yard and enhances the beauty of the adobe buildings.

The passionflower blossom, with its many symbolic parts.

This restored fountain at the Santa Inez mission is characteristic of those which might have been created at ranchos. The low profile allows access by livestock and wildlife.

The simplicity of this fountain and the statue of a saint at the center is simple yet effective in this palm and succulent courtyard.

Spanish tile fountain.

The walls of this adobe home illustrate its earthen color and texture. This wall beneath the veranda is exposed only because it is protected by the roof from rain and wind.

These steps show the wide variety of glazed tile colors and patterns available today.

This wall suggests adobe but is actually constructed of very old brick and covered with white-washed plaster.

More contemporary walls are constructed of stucco, or unit masonry beneath a smooth layer of plaster. The gate is beautifully crafted and finished with a turquoise hue.

In early gardens, potted plants were frequently collected around water sources for convenience.

Terra-cotta pots allow vines to grow upon veranda posts when there are no openings in the pavement for plants.

mahogany bed simply too much for their exhausted oxen. No doubt with tear-stained faces, these women watched their family heirlooms gradually disappear, shimmering in the heat waves of the desert.

But although they could do without the furniture, these precious seeds and roots were never relinquished. When the family finally settled down, the plants represented all that was left of their old life, with fragrance and brightly colored flowers harking many memories back to many cherished times. These first plants were most often cultivated close to the house, where browsing wildlife and farm animals were less likely to sample the foliage. These were not plantings for the sake of prettiness but strictly for utility, and if a plant did have an attractive flower, then all the better.

Over time the plants would require protection, so a paling or picket fence would be erected. Early on, such a barrier would simply be a row of sticks inserted into the ground and attached along the top. The material varied with what was available in each region. On California's north coast, heart redwood was plentiful and easily split into fencing for sheep pasture. The wood was resistant to decay, and most are still in use today—contributing to the area's unique landscape character. In southern California and inland deserts, sticks even

𝒜 prosperous farm with a well-tended dooryard garden of hollyhocks and flowering vines. (*Community Memorial Museum*)

the thorny petioles of native palm fronds went into fencing. Eventually, highly ornamental milled pickets replaced these rustic but functional fences, but the purpose was always the same: to enclose the dooryard garden.

As the homestead grew, this space provided a safe enclosure for young children, away from horses, wagons, and other livestock. The yard was carpeted in thrifty, deep-rooted pasture grasses that developed into thick, soft clumps along with blooming clovers. If the grass grew too long, a lamb or calf could be staked out for a day in the garden for a thorough mowing. Today there is a movement to return to this sort of agrarian "pasture-grass lawn," which is more environmentally friendly than highly bred turf grasses. Also within the fence, flowers appeared, their brilliant colors relatively even more stunning in that era of natural dyes, when precious factory-dyed cloth would be faded by the sun and brutal treatment from washboards and harsh lye soap.

The earliest nursery establishments in the West catered to their customer's preference for plants they knew well back East. These would include the fragrant lilac, with roses and honeysuckle to drape upon porch roofs. But since growers were often far from home, natives such as redbud, California lilac, yucca, and a bevy of wildflowers often appeared in the dooryard.

Finally, the single most important factor that separated the Mexican era of agriculture from that of the Americans in California was the advent of irrigation and drainage. The tules died out when ditches drained the valley lowlands. Sierra river water was diverted into flumes and ditches to supply irrigation to both the foothills and the valley farms. Deeper wells at many sites were far more reliable in dry years than the fickle springs of the missions and ranchos. Over time the great water projects of southern California supported the miraculous transformation of a desertlike landscape to miles of citrus groves and row crops.

Farming was one of California's three major industries, mining and timber being the other two, beginning in the 1850s. The demand for improved varieties of crops better suited to our climate was relentless, and the noted horticulturist Luther Burbank sought to fill the needs. His life's work in Sonoma County breeding plants was of infinite value to the state, and his name can never be separated from local agricultural history.

Today agriculture is still thriving in our mild climate and deep

soils, and it will forever be the heart and soul of the state. It is threatened only by a rising population's constant demand to develop fertile
land near cities into residential subdivisions. This, coupled with controversy over the environment and methods of commercial farming,
may eventually deprive future generations of the great agricultural
heritage of California.

THE FLORA OF THE NEW SETTLERS

Common Lilac
Syringa vulgaris

The lilac is an old plant in garden terms, first cultivated during
the 1500s when it was introduced to Europe from the Far East via
Turkey. The lilac is known chiefly for its potently scented flowers. It
is very large as shrubs go, nearing treelike proportions when mature.
Its tolerance of extremely cold winters is seen in the fact that during
the early 1800s virtually every French-Canadian dooryard had at least
one lilac. It was also well-loved by New Englanders and is the official
state flower of New Hampshire.

Kate Wolf, the late folk songwriter of the Sierra foothills, wrote
poignantly of this shrub in her sad and haunting song "The Lilac and
the Apple." This song vividly describes the site of a long-abandoned
farmhouse tucked away on a sunny, south-facing slope where a lilac
still grew and bloomed although no one came to see. In fact, the presence of isolated lilac shrubs in the countryside are sometimes the only
indicator that a home was once located there. This tenacity is why the
lilac was so much a part of the Old West, for it could be depended
upon to survive more cold and drought than any other plant that
hailed from the East. And no doubt pioneers found some comfort in
seeing these colorful, sweetly scented blooms in their new, arid
homesites.

Because many immigrants came not only from the East but
Europe as well, they brought tales of lilac folklore that increased its
appeal. Lilacs are often associated with luck, and anyone who finds a
white lilac blossom with five petals instead of four is granted "lilac-
luck," a belief similar to that concerning four-leaf clovers. The lilac
has always been considered a guardian of the house, and peasants of

eastern Europe afraid of lightning often tried to protect their homes from a strike by placing a sprig of lilac on the roof.

To the English, a girl could wear lilac blossoms only on May Day; if she wore it at any other time, she would never wear a wedding ring. On a darker note, lilac was also associated with death and illness, appearing frequently in old poems. This connection likely originated with the flowers' scent being as potent as that of sage, which must have been an effective means of pleasantly masking offensive odors of the sickroom and the grave.

The common lilac is available in a variety of cultivars, with flowers ranging from pure white to the deepest purple. It prefers a cold winter and may not grow vigorously or bloom well in mild southern California and adjoining states. The lilac is one of the backbone shrubs of any rural garden, and a drive through the countryside during its early spring bloom period reveals how prevalent it really is.

Weeping Willow
Salix babylonica

All willows are riparian species native to riverbanks, lakeshores, lowlands, or where ground water is unusually high. The weeping willow, with its graceful, pendulous tresses of foliage, is the consummate farm pond tree. It is far larger and more picturesque than the native scrub willows of the West, but this and most other willows are quick to sprout from cuttings. They have large, invasive root systems capable of destroying paving and underground utilities. It is unfortunate that most urban and suburban homesites are too small for this aggressive tree, but on farms and ranches it is totally in scale with its surroundings, and most attractive when viewed from a suitable distance.

The weeping willow, *Salix babylonica*, originated in China, but Europeans thought it was from the Holy Land and thus named it after the Gardens of Babylon. In the 1700s the potter Thomas Minton depicted the tree in his first blue plates, which would be forever named "willow-ware." His inspiration, during an era when Asian art was popular, came from a Chinese legend of lovers eloping over a bridge beneath the boughs of a weeping willow tree. In Europe the trees first grown in England, and those early individuals in the Colonies were always vastly popular, as the unique and attractive form was in great demand. The ease of propagation made it widely available throughout America (and George Washington wrote of it), spanning the continent to the West, where its rapid growth promised much-needed shade in a relatively short period.

The branches and shoots of the weeping willow grow long and thin, yet are strong and flexible. Farmers planted the trees for utilitarian purposes, and even today in Europe the weeping willows are severely cut back each year to encourage a crop of whiplike growth. This technique, called coppicing, was also practiced by American farmers, who cut in the early spring, when the sap first began to flow but before leaves became a hindrance.

There were dozens of uses for this rank willow growth around the homestead. When metal baling wire was a luxury, willow whips were used to bind together split rail fences. If wrapped and knotted tightly while still green, they hardened as they dried and became quite durable. Bent willow furniture originated in the pioneer days of America and became widespread, with the artistic twig furniture of the late nineteenth century the pinnacle of this primitive craft. Willow has always been a basic material for both Native American and Anglo basket makers throughout the Far West. Ben Franklin was known to comment on some willow baskets he saw on the wharf in Pennsylvania, which had sprouted leaves. He remarked how durable a plant it must be to take to such contorted shapes yet remain living.

It is interesting to note that when burned, the charcoal of willow wood was considered the best for making gunpowder. Shoots of willow cut in early spring, when the bark slipped off easily, revealed clean, white wood. Willow shoots stripped this way made the famous willow whistles, a popular toy for homestead children—hence the expression "clean as a whistle." The image of the weeping willow has also been a common sight on pioneer gravestones, for as the tree wept in form, so did the mourners. Willows may also symbolize life after death, because they persist in regrowing even after brutal treatment that would have killed any other type of tree.

In nineteenth-century America it was a common practice to plant willows beside roadways that passed through marshy, wet ground. The willow's appetite for water sent its extensive, fibrous root system through the soil to harden the ground of the roadbed and bind it so that wagon wheels might pass over with less sinking. Secondly, the roots drew water out of the surrounding soil to dry it more quickly. This was also the cause for weeping willows to be planted with various poplars and alders along the banks of streams, rivers, and earth dams. There they discouraged soil erosion from rapidly moving water by binding soil with their roots.

John C. Frémont's Famous Cottonwood
Populus fremontii

John C. Frémont was dubbed "the Pathfinder," yet he proved to have difficulties getting around California, despite the already established trails used by traders and Indian tribes. So poor was he at travel planning, he nearly starved to death crossing the Sierra Nevada in winter while on an expedition to map local routes. But despite various fiascos, even including a court-martial, he remains a notable historic character for his efforts to survey and map much of the state. During these expeditions, his detailed notes on native vegetation proved quite accurate, and as a result, the western cottonwood as well as several other plants bear his name today.

In 1844 Frémont, along with Kit Carson and others of the expedition, camped beneath a grove of trees beside Pyramid Lake, Nevada. Frémont wrote about them that night in January as being similar to the cottonwoods he knew from the Great Plains, where Native Americans fed their horses on the bark during winter. Frémont referred to these Far West cottonwoods as "sweet" because his own horses fed upon its bark, which kept them from starving in the barren desert. In April he wrote of finding the same trees in the San Joaquin Valley as well as in dry washes of the Mohave Desert. He would come to the conclusion that the presence of these cottonwoods indicated a water source, even though the surrounding terrain might be barren. In the porous sands of the desert, rivers often flow underground and feed these giant trees. Perhaps the best examples of this are the groves at the bottom of the Grand Canyon.

Frémont cottonwood was an often-used hanging tree, as it might be the only tree for miles in the desert towns of eastern California, Nevada, and Arizona. The most famous is the Hanging Cottonwood of Genoa, Nevada, which was used by a lynch mob to execute a drifter who shot a local Mormon resident. After the deed the townspeople felt so guilty, they sawed off the hanging branch, and the tree was never used again.

In the small Gold Rush town of Rough and Ready, California, an unusual tale surrounds one of these cottonwoods. This town was so independent that in the 1850s, when statehood was achieved, the town citizens refused to comply with the new state government. In order to continue their riotous behavior, the miners seceded from the Union, although not permanently. In just a few days after taking over the post office, the independent mining camp finally agreed to join the Union with the rest of the state. Among the many tales coming out of this mining district is one about the origin of a massive cottonwood that stood in the middle of town well into the twentieth century.

The story of its planting begins during the Gold Rush, when a beautiful slave woman was brought to town by a local miner. She was quite a horsewoman and would break off switches from trees to lash her mounts on to greater speeds. Leaping from her horse one day, she thrust the switch into the ground, and there it stayed to root and grow into an enormous specimen.

The genus *Populus* was named as such because the shoots and twigs would root quickly if anyone simply pushed them into the soil, like the switch of the slave woman. Virtually any member of the population could grow trees of the genus *Populus*. But fast growth results in notoriously weak branching, and the tops of very old trees are often irregular from wind damage. If mature limbs fall, they can cause serious damage, so these trees are not recommended for sites close to buildings unless pruned for strength. The cottonwood attained its common name from the fluffy, white fibers attached to its seed. The slightest breeze will cause the seed to be disbursed as the cotton falls like a summer snowstorm. This, and the typical invasive rooting of a riparian tree, makes it a poor candidate for a cultivated garden. However, the fast growth and beauty of poplars (the common name for any tree of the genus) for Western farms and ranches has produced a new generation of hybrid poplars, or what many prefer to call the cottonless cottonwoods. George Zappetini, a retired forester in Sonora, California, has experimented with numerous cultivars and has discovered what he considers the perfect tree. It has no cotton and may be planted from unrooted poles anywhere from twelve inches long to as much as twenty feet. Prices are very low since they are shipped only during the winter bareroot season, which makes them inexpensive solutions for large properties. The long poles result in practically instant trees, as they leaf out the first year.

Because poplars have such fibrous root systems, they become potbound very quickly. Once transplanted, the roots are slow to venture into new soil. The poles are simply planted in a posthole or shoved down into moist soils, as the pioneers did. The poles are guar-

A northern California farmhouse with vines shrouding the front porch and clustered along fence lines. (*California State Library*)

anteed to root if provided with sufficient water. A single mother tree on a site may produce dozens of poles each year if coppiced a few feet above the ground. Trees tend to produce a large number of suckers from stumps, which every year or two may be harvested to allow for a new crop. A large piece of land may be reforested with the suckers literally for free. In many cases these poplars are planted along with slower maturing species, so the poplars provide immediate shading. When the slower species mature, the poplars may be cut down and used for firewood or cut into poles for new trees.

Honeysuckle
Lonicera japonica

Honeysuckle is a fast-growing evergreen vine that blooms for much of the summer with tiny, trumpet-shaped flowers that are white when the buds open, then yellow as each matures. There are two reasons why honeysuckle was so prevalent on Western homesteads. As with the lilac, plants with potent fragrance were an effective means of masking odors before deodorants and perfume. The honeysuckle flowers are so intensely sweet that they also draw large numbers of hummingbirds and bees to pollinate food crops. Perhaps we all have pulled the petals of the flowers from the sepals in order to taste the drop of nectar that was hidden deep inside (and no doubt the children on these early farms did).

Japanese honeysuckle was available during the middle of the nineteenth century. It sprouts easily from seed, and as settlers gradually moved westward, their beloved, fragrant honeysuckle went with them. Throughout the Midwest the vine has naturalized and is now a serious pest due to the incredible number of seedlings produced each year. With this kind of large-scale reproduction, recessive genes for greater frost-tolerance have appeared, and the invasion is slowly moving northward. Eventually it will threaten the northern hardwood forests.

In the dry West, honeysuckle's durable, forgiving nature made it one of the few garden plants that could survive the heat and drought. And the bonus of profuse, highly scented flowers was particularly important. It was planted upon fence lines, walls of houses, and porch awnings. Because it grew fast and covered so well, honeysuckle also became used as a groundcover, developing into large mounds shrouding anything in its path. Today this quality makes it a good slope-stabilizing plant to discourage surface erosion.

But honeysuckle also has a secret night life, for it is pollinated by moths. The beloved characteristics of the flowers act in different ways to attract night flying moths through light, scent, and nectar. Its white and pale yellow flower colors reflect the light of the moon to make them easier for the moths to find in the darkness, and, as we all know, moths cannot resist drawing close to light sources at night. The potent fragrance can reach the moths over long distances to help pull them in, and it also indicates that the flower contains nectar, which is food for the moths. Finally, the moths are rewarded with nectar, which is obtained while hovering at the mouth of the flower. The moth's "tongue" reaches down deep into the tubular petals, brushing against the noticeably protruding anthers for a dusting of pollen.

Before planting honeysuckle in today's country gardens, consider its eventual size, which is enormous. If it tends to reseed itself, be cautious, because our fragile Western ecosystems, particularly forests and riparian habitats, are vulnerable to its rampant spread. This illustrates the irony of gardening with drought-tolerant plants. A species capable of surviving well on very little water and exhibits vigorous growth under this condition is a first-rate candidate for a dry garden.

However, it may be even better adapted to California than our own native species and thus eventually will replace them. This problem occurs with other common plants as well, and care should be taken if a garden site is adjacent to wildlands or when dumping garden refuse in the vicinity of these lands.

An important aspect of honeysuckle in the landscape is that it tends to produce a large amount of twiggy growth, then grows further upon this layer to reach plenty of sunlight. The mound will grow taller each year, with new shoots reaching upward beyond last year's foliage. This creates a mammoth cleanup job if vines are not thinned out annually. Certainly a few well-placed flowering runners espaliered to an arbor or fence are far more attractive than a sea of impenetrable vine.

Oleander
Nerium oleander

There are strips of older highway throughout California that were lined with oleander shrubs to create a drought-tolerant, deep green, leafy wall of plants. They help to absorb sound, block headlights, and reduce heat island effects of blacktop. And when blooming in great masses of delicious watermelon pinks, lipstick red, and white, there is nothing as typically Western nor as resistant to adversity. Yet no plant is so widely taken for granted.

The oleander originated in the Middle East, where it grows on the banks of dry streambeds that contain water for only a short time each year. It was believed to have appeared in Spain after the Crusades, and it eventually made it to the American West. Of no religious, medicinal, or food value, it was not often cultivated at the missions, but it was appreciated for its color alone in Mexico. During the American settling of California, the shrub proved to solve a variety of problems, but most of all it brightened the dooryard gardens even when denied water for long periods.

One story originating from the Caribbean island of Bermuda attempts to explain the naming of the oleander. It begins with the first plants—then called the South Sea rose—brought from Europe to the New World in 1800. A maiden of the islands had a lover named Leander who was a sailor. When Leander went to sea, he promised to marry her in the parish church upon his return. The maiden wept for a long time after their parting. Each day when the tide turned and ships could approach the island, she sat under her pink South Sea rose to watch for the sails. But when news came that the ship had been lost, she cried, "Oh, Leander, oh, Leander" beneath the pink flowers forevermore. This charming legend is probably not the true source of the name. More likely it is based on the similarity of oleander foliage to that of the olive, whose genus is *Olea*.

Oleander hedges are evergreen, dense, and quite capable of blocking wind. Tolerant of the extreme heat of Arabian deserts, the plants are good barriers in our own inland deserts. They have long been essential to stop blowing sand and protect more sensitive garden plants behind them. Desert winds not only dry foliage but pit and tatter it, yet the rigid, leathery leaves of oleander are virtually immune. The plants also make excellent screens to block unsightly areas within a yard or outside the property line. They can be planted, sheared, and trained into a flowering gateway on a par with England's box or beech hedges.

Oleanders are highly poisonous plants, and all parts should be considered toxic. Even when burned, its smoke carries the toxin, and water used for cut flowers of oleanders can become equally nasty. In fact, Europeans use the plant as rat poison. Interestingly enough, the plant kills horses, but apparently goats may browse upon it with no ill effects, although this is not proven a general fact, as individual goats and plants do vary somewhat.

For residents native to California, it's common to literally hate oleanders, just as some cannot abide palms. They are often considered freeway plants and nothing else. But what other plant will promise backyard privacy in just a few years? How many shrubs will regrow so vigorously after a novice prunes it back to a bare stub? Which plant will leaf out right down to the ground and never show its legs if left untouched? And finally, are there any other large shrubs that make good standard trees and dwarf flowering hedges as well? Think about it next time the water in your neighborhood is rationed and your neighbor's oleanders are blooming like crazy while your roses wilt and promptly die.

Scouring Rush
Equisetum hyemale

You'll find them growing along roadsides, in drainage ditches, and in meadows along the coast or those at higher elevations of the Sierra Nevada. In fact, it is native to just about every state from the

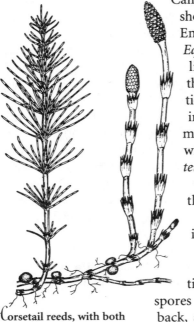

𝒽orsetail reeds, with both fertile and infertile stems and connecting roots.

Canadian border to Mexico and has even shown up in the medieval gardens of England. This adaptable reed is *Equisetum*, very ancient form of plant life that has managed to survive through 400 million years of evolution. During the first quarter of that, in the Devonian period, there were many different species of this plant, with one relative, *Equisetum giganteum*, reaching over thirty feet tall.

Only a few species exist today, and they are quite normal in size. However, scouring rush is still a living fossil with an unusual life cycle. It sends out its first shoots in spring: slender rods topped by cone-shaped tips that contain its spores. After the spores are released, these fertile rods die back, and a second, infertile set grows in their place, bearing a distinctly different, bottlebrush appearance.

Due to the antiquity of this plant, it carries a number of different common names that are based on various unique features, as it is very primitive and resembles a rich, but soft green, segmented bamboo. Its genus name, *Equisetum*, refers to the infertile rods accented with whorls of needlelike leaves protruding from the joint of each segment. These leaves can grow quite long and resemble a bottlebrush, or in the eyes of our ancestors, a horse's tail. Hence comes the root of the genus name *equis*, and the common name, horsetail or bottlebrush. Another feature is that the plant's cells contain a high amount of silica, which makes them abrasive. When bundled together, they made a durable brush used for centuries for scrubbing implements, which explains the origin of its other common name, scouring rush. During the Middle Ages in Europe it was called yet another name, pewterwort, because the silica could shine pewter without scratching.

This was a valuable plant to Western pioneer women, who gathered horsetails in wet places. While on the trail, women collected when they could, bundled the stoutly cut reeds, and stored them for future use. Due to its widespread distribution, it was known by people of all extractions. The California Native Americans found the flexible reeds could be collapsed into a ribbon for sand paper. While an arrow shaft was held upright between the knees, the ribbon was wrapped around the wood, then pulled back and forth in a sawing motion. Horsetail has also been used as a survival food, but only under threat of starvation, because it contains some alkaloids that influence the digestive system. The outer tissue of young shoots is removed, the inner core is eaten raw, and it is said to have a mildly sweet taste.

Horsetails are also an interesting plant to use in gardens. Because of its primitive survival ability, it dies back completely in the dry season, only to come forth again when moisture is sufficient. It is frost-tolerant and more attractive than many forms of bamboo, in a refreshing shade of green. I have seen it growing in terra-cotta pots to lend an exotic quality for very little effort. Like bamboo, it spreads by underground stems and can become invasive. Being a native plant, however, it presents no threat to the local ecosystems.

It's difficult, but not impossible, to find horsetails for sale in the nursery. The best way to bring it to your garden is to transplant from wild stands in a waste area such as roadsides, then dig out enough to include some root. As the shoots die out, cut them off so new, greener ones can take their places, and be sure to give it enough moisture in the dry summer months.

Landmark Palms
Washingtonia filifera, Washingtonia robusta, Phoenix canariensis

Homesites of the early pioneers still dot the fertile valleys of California. Some are beautifully restored, and others are long forgotten, with only the most rugged plants to indicate they were ever there at all. An interesting phenomenon concerning these sites has become an integral part of the aesthetic of our Golden State: Palm trees have lingered behind, almost as monuments to earlier settlement. After many years of careful observation, I have found that a large number of the old places are marked by a single palm, usually a Mexican or California fan palm. Why do these two species predominate, and why only one individual to a site?

A very early nineteenth-century map of Colusa County and the Sutter Buttes, showing only a few "wagon" roads across the valley, provided the clue. The land was incredibly flat and is still dense with tall tule growth, oak groves, riparian forests, and orchards. Travelers unfamiliar with the area would have a difficult time finding a home-site due to the limited visibility. Even locals, confused by tule fog, darkness, or stormy weather, may also have become disoriented. But the single very tall palm foliage head rising clearly above the surrounding vegetation would serve as a point of reference, a landmark because it resembled no other tree.

A second factor leading to the planting of palms is their ability, like a cactus, to retain moisture within their trunks. Small palms could be easily transplanted by farmers with practically no rootball to speak of and yet survive. Although the Mexican fan palm grew faster, the California fan palm was more resistant to the rare hard freezes that hit the state. As a result, the majority of these homestead palms that remain in the northern portion of the state today are the California natives, while in the warmer southern portion of the San Joaquin Valley, the Mexican species is more prevalent.

Eddie Hanlin, a surveyor at MHM, a Marysville engineering firm that dates back to the 1800s, believes that palms served yet another purpose that actually did make them official landmarks. After a farmer had his land surveyed, he often marked corners and lines by planting palms. This is why sometimes a single tree or a line of them can be found out in the middle of nowhere. During a time when far more valley land was still marshy and undeveloped, a survey stake or marker could easily be lost, but the column of a palm trunk not only was easy to find, but it would not be confused with surrounding vegetation.

There are a few other reasons for the frequency of palms in the California rural landscape. Often rubbish piles where household garbage was dumped sprouted palm trees from discarded parlor palms or date pits. Amateur archaeologists long used this relationship to find buried bottle dumps. Many species of palms also reseed themselves at surprising rates. Old fan palms planted as street trees in downtown Sacramento each rise out of a five-foot square opening in the sidewalk. All around the base are dozens of seedlings that public works officials must control or they will develop into quite a thicket. Where an old farmhouse palm was successful in fruiting, the chances of its creating numerous offspring was very likely. Some of the fruits were no doubt carried off by the birds, others gobbled up by barnyard animals, and distributed in a far-off pasture.

LUTHER BURBANK

I firmly believe, from what I have seen, that this is the chosen spot of all this earth as far as Nature is concerned.

LUTHER BURBANK
on arrival in Santa Rosa in 1875

At the height of his career, they called Luther Burbank the "Plant Wizard," and indeed he must have seemed like Merlin himself while producing over 800 new plants through careful, selective breeding. Burbank (1849–1926) was born in New England and as a young man read Darwin's book *Variation of Animals and Plants under Domestication*, which introduced him to the concept of natural selection. During that time, Darwin's theories were hotly debated against interpretations of Biblical creation accounts, and this conflict would persist through much of Burbank's life. Burbank would later claim this book was the single work that opened up a new world and set his mind on the road to selective plant breeding.

Luther Burbank began farming in the 1870s while in New England, where a stroke of luck pushed him into the plant breeding business. The potato famine of Europe had spread to America. Disease virtually wiped out the older, established varieties, leaving only an inferior yet disease-resistant strain imported from Chile as a replacement. This fostered great demand for a better potato, but since the plants are generally reproduced only by tubers and do not set seed, there was no way to unlock the gene pool to find better cultivars. One miraculous day Burbank found a single seed ball on one of his potato plants, rare because potatoes were not known to produce seed. He allowed it to mature and obtained twenty-three nearly microscopic seeds that he planted at his farm. Out of the plants which resulted, he was to select only two which were superior to any currently

Luther Burbank.

in cultivation. Burbank sold part of this revolutionary potato crop to a farmer, who labeled the new variety the "Burbank Seedling"—the ancestor and close relation of our famous Idaho russets.

Lured by relatives who wrote home about the wondrous agricultural climate of California, Burbank sold his farm in the East and came to Santa Rosa in 1875 with his precious seed potatoes. The town was little more than a village and in the grips of a recession. He planted some of his white-fleshed potatoes on a friend's farm in Tomales; it failed commercially because Californians did not want a white potato at the time, but it later became widespread. Burbank finally found work at a Petaluma nursery until the economy improved, when his mother and sister came West to live with him. Together they bought a four-acre site, where Burbank raised fruits and vegetables in his spare time.

Local growers scoffed at a Petaluma banker's request for supply of 20,000 prune trees in a single season. Rising to the occasion, Burbank claimed he could fill the order. He did so through a method of grafting called June-budding, where he bud grafted prune wood onto almond rootstocks. When the banker found that Burbank had indeed met the challenge, he deemed him the Plant Wizard. This was the beginning of Burbank's work with plums, and he is credited with over one hundred other varieties, many so well suited to the California climate that they are widely cultivated today.

This event produced a cash flow that allowed Burbank to enter the plant business full-time, and he purchased a larger, eighteen-acre site in Sebastopol, some miles to the west of Santa Rosa. There he began large-scale breeding and testing of newly introduced plants from around the world. His basic method was to cross plants and sow the seed in immense numbers, up to 10,000 individuals. He would then assess each one for particular qualities he was looking for, and of this original planting only 50 to 100 were preserved, the rest burned. This process of elimination would continue until Burbank found a plant to his liking.

Burbank had no formal science or horticultural education. Many in the scientific community criticized him for his methods, such as keeping no technical records to document the breeding process. Academics labeled him a charlatan, yet his efforts successfully resulted in rapid development of new varieties of plants that were better suited to the California climate than their predecessors from the East. Burbank always maintained his dedication to the goal of creating more productive plants to feed the world, a humanitarian effort for which he was honored with a $10,000 Carnegie grant to fund research five years in a row. Unfortunately, a representative of the grant program visited Burbank, found the record-keeping practically nonexistent, and denied renewal of the grant.

It is important to realize that during this time there were no plant patents as there are today. A plant patent credits the breeder who first introduced the plant, preventing others from propagating or selling the plant without permission from the patent holder. But Burbank's new varieties were not protected this way, and a new variety was simply sold as parent material to other growers. His 1893 catalog, "New Creations in Plants and Flowers," offered 250 exclusive Burbank plants to growers at prices well over $1,000 apiece. This high price acted like a plant patent for a while, because only the grower who bought first from Burbank had the material to sell. But once the plants were propagated and sold to the public, there was no more control over resale.

The later part of Luther Burbank's life was a time of both great successes and dismal failures. He was often visited by important public figures, such as Helen Keller, President Taft, William Jennings Bryan, Henry Ford, Thomas Edison, and John Muir. Burbank often disagreed with the religious community regarding evolution and natural selection, and a great controversy arose about his writings on human eugenics. The human eugenics movement of the nineteenth century suggested that humans, just as plants, could be selectively bred to promote beneficial traits, while undesirable characteristics could be weeded out. His beliefs placed him in a bad light and was often the object of scorn in the national media.

Luther Burbank died on April 11, 1926, at age 77. It is said there were 5,000 people at his funeral. He asked that he be buried beneath the cedar of Lebanon tree in front of the cottage where he and his second wife had lived. Upon her death in 1977, the house and grounds in Santa Rosa were granted to the city and are now the Luther Burbank Home and Gardens. Luther Burbank was California's most noted horticulturist, a true plant wizard who, with little more than a strong will, limitless tenacity, and great vision, single-handedly created an entire world of new plants perfectly adapted to the West.

Some of Luther Burbank's Most Famous Introductions
List courtesy of Luther Burbank Home and Gardens, Santa Rosa, California.

'Burbank' Potato	Shasta Daisy hybrids
'Elephant' Garlic	'Burbank Crimson' California Poppy

The Tragedy of the American Elm

The older neighborhoods of the city of Sacramento are generously shaded by the spreading canopies of massive American elms (Ulmus americana). They are monstrous trees, with canopies rising far above the tallest three-story Victorians that line these old streets. Planning by the early city fathers lined the avenues with elms, which were easily rooted and grew vigorously on the high water table beneath the city. Today, well over a hundred years later, many of the trees still stand.

A heat island is a condition where the combined reflected heat of paved surfaces, masonry, and buildings raises the city temperature far above normal. There is a movement to bring more trees to cities in order to reduce the heat island effect and improve air quality. Perhaps the best way to see just how effective shade trees can be is to visit the old neighborhoods of Sacramento on a hot summer day. There is a profound difference in ambient air temperatures beneath the shade trees of downtown than in the lower density yet much hotter suburbs to the east.

It is tragic that these majestic old elms are now fac-

'Santa Rosa' Plum	'Burbank Admiral' Pea
'Himalaya' Blackberry	'Paradox' Walnut
'Satsuma' Plum	'Royal' Walnut
'Lemon Giant' Calla Lily	'Phenomenal' Berry
'Iceberg' White Blackberry	'Tarrytown' Canna
'Burbank' Rose	'Crimson Winter' Rhubarb
'Wickson' Plum	'Mayflower' Fragrant Verbena
'Santa Rosa' Dahlia	'Burbank' Cherry
'Robusta' Strawberry	'Sebastopol' Thornless Blackberry
'July Elberta' Peach	'Tower-of-Gold' *Kniphofia*
'Black Giant' Cherry	'Santa Rosa Strain' Shirley Poppies
Hybrid Watsonias	Hybrid Sunflowers
Spineless *Opuntia* Cacti	Plumcots, cross of plum with apricot

ing disease and pestilence so great there is little that can be done to save them. The elm leaf beetle, a very small insect, afflicts the trees in heavy populations every summer. They consume leaf tissue to the extent that the entire tree may defoliate before the middle of summer. As if this were not enough, Dutch elm disease is also destroying elms. It is spread by the elm bark beetle, which bores through the cambium layer beneath the bark to cut off water and nutrient transportation. There is no simple treatment for the disease, and so feared is it that this and other vulnerable species of trees are now strictly quarantined. No longer can we plant and enjoy American elms in California, and as the last mature specimens die out, they will be the end.

There is much to learn from this sad situation. Landscape architects stress the importance of planting a diversity of species, not just a single type of tree, no matter how hardy and picturesque. Such was the mistake in Sacramento, and had the early planners known about Dutch elm disease and beetles, they might have combined the elms with a number of other tree species.

Country Roses

There is no doubt that some of the roses on immigrant farms originated from the old species at mission or rancho sites. But during the middle of the nineteenth century, rose breeding was very popular in the Eastern states, and examples of Eastern varieties have been found on some of the early California farm sites, with massive trunks and foliage covering an area sixty feet in diameter. A popular yellow variety introduced in 1830 was 'Harrison's Yellow', which at one time could be found in virtually any garden in the East. It is thought that this would be the most likely candidate to be carried across the plains in a covered wagon, as yellow is not a common flower color in species roses. Other well-loved varieties of this period include 'Lamarque', 'Niphetos', 'Safrano', 'Duchess de Brabant', and 'Beauty of Glazenwood'.

Roses were quicker to catch on in southern California, although it was far more sparsely populated. The warm weather increased the blooming season to almost year-round, a miracle that drew rose aficionados from all points. The mild winters also eliminated the need for severe pruning; without the annual blunt cutting, the plants grew to magnificent proportions.

As a result, the Los Angeles basin and its environs became the center of commercial rose production for the West Coast. As early as 1855, horticulturist W.B. Osborne had for sale nearly one hundred different varieties, most from the East, but others no doubt of mission origin. This was even more remarkable when it was discovered he tended over twenty thousand plants in Los Angeles, which at that time was still just slightly more than a dusty Mexican pueblo.

The roses of Los Angeles began to take on legendary proportions, and lovers of this "queen of flowers" flocked to the area to view General Stonemans' tree rose 'Lamarque', with a trunk fifteen inches thick and the crown twenty feet tall. A specimen of 'Beauty of Glazenwood' in the same area actually covered an eighty-foot-tall eucalyptus tree, transforming it into a giant pillar of blooms. Another great rose was a hedge of climbing 'Gold of Ophir' that stretched over a mile from a single plant.

Perhaps no other part of the American West was supplied with as many different varieties early on as California. We can assume this reliable and vigorous flower was widely traded, and the mammoth examples detailed above no doubt stimulated horticulturally minded farmers to cultivate their own 'Beauty of Glazenwood' or 'Lamarque'. These early specimens were appreciated for their rare beauty on the isolated farm, where the fragrance was precious. Plants draped themselves over fences, softened porches, or simply mounded into soft clouds of flowers. These were the simple dooryard roses of the pioneers, sometimes joined by native roses and the species of the missions.

Wild Fruits

Even today, picking blackberries by the wayside is a popular summer activity, but it was even more so in the early days, when there were few if any fruit trees on isolated homesteads. California abounds with wild fruits, many of which were enjoyed only by the native people, but a number were also relished by immigrants.

Wild plum (*Prunus subcordata*) is native to the Coast Ranges and Sierra Nevada foothills. It produces small, red plums that were eaten fresh or preserved as jelly. To gold miners at isolated placer claims, these fruits were a precious source of vitamins to reduce the symptoms of scurvy and gave variety to a diet of salt pork, parched corn, and dried beans. Many old timers still prefer plums of the Sierra to cultivated ones. The esteemed botanist Dr. W.L. Jepson of the University of California noted that this native plum tended to vary considerably, with some trees producing quite tasty fruit but others producing fruit so sour as to be inedible. Mr. Felix Gillet of Nevada City grafted improved plums onto rootstocks of native plums; he found the root systems proved to be larger, but there resulted no other advantages.

These are not to be confused with seedlings of cultivated plums, which began cropping up in the later nineteenth century and do not often take on the characteristics of their more civilized parent. These are called seed plums because they mature to about the size of a large marble and consist mostly of seed, with a thin but very sweet flesh.

The wild blackberry (*Rubus vitifolius*) is both a blessing and a curse to California. Its thorny, invasive runners can displace valuable pasture and farmland at incredible speed. But it is so prolific there was always plenty of fruit left over after the women and children went picking. It was so esteemed by early pioneers that Luther Burbank extensively hybridized the blackberry into more productive varieties, although the native was certainly generous with its fruit. It was also the ancestor of the modern Loganberry.

Today the vines often grow along irrigation ditches and road-sides, where there is more water during the summer months. It is a common practice for highway crews and farmers to spray the plants with herbicides to check growth, which makes fruit produced in these areas risky to pick. One should not pick from plants with any with-ered leaves or distorted or discolored growth, or from plants that seem unhealthy in any way. Even with this common knowledge, peo-ple can be found gathering from the shoulders of rural roads despite apparent herbicide damage.

Settlers in the northern California forests were often called stump farmers because the stumps of the massive trees would linger in their fields for so long. Lurking in this moist environment is the huckleberry (*Vaccinium ovatum*) which is closely related to and resembles the blueberry. It was preserved or eaten fresh by pioneers. In fact, one year as many as two thousand boxes were documented to have been profitably gathered in the hills of western Sonoma County.

Fruit Trees: The Farmer's Stock and Trade

Today orchards blanket large portions of the Sacramento and San Joaquin valleys. These fruit and nut crops are highly productive, with harvest rates far greater than those in the East. Although early fruit trees were gleaned from secularized mission plantings, some of the first immigrant farmers brought with them what they considered their most important possessions: seeds and seedlings. Martin Lelong came to California in 1846 with a small lot of French apple varieties growing in a box, which he planted in Los Angeles. The fruit tree industry began a bit later in 1849 when W.H. Nash and R.L. Kilburn arranged for a nursery in New York to ship a box of six fruit trees around Cape Horn during winter while dormant and packed in damp moss. They survived and were planted in Napa Valley in 1850. The apple varieties included Rhode Island Greening, Roxbury Russet, Winesap, Red Romanite, and Esopus Spoitzenburg. Also shipped were Bartlett and Seckel pears, as well as Black Tartarian and Napoleon Bigarreau cherries.

Another early effort were the apple trees of Peter Weimar, who planted seeds he took from dried apples shipped from the East. These did well in the fertile banks of the American River and developed into profitable trees during the Gold Rush, when fresh fruit sold for sky high prices.

Despite these early enterprises, farm orchards were actually called fruit gardens. It was believed at first that frequent and heavy watering of the trees was essential, due to the arid climate and long growing season. As a result, trees planted with the needs of water supply in mind covered only a minimal area, but at high density.

During the middle 1850s this belief in heavy irrigation caused dwarf root stocks to be hailed for best production because more trees could be packed into each acre of orchard. Dwarf pear and apple fruit gardens covered much of what is now our major northern California inland cities. A Mr. Fountain cultivated three acres in Oakland that were planted with an astounding 1,600 dwarf apple and pear trees.

The farmers who grew their trees for commercial fruit production and not just for home use faced a new climate with highly fickle rainfall patterns. There were no rainfall or temperature records to consult to predict dates of harvest or fruit set. The potential for fungus, virus, and pest invasions were also discovered through the process of trial and error. As a result, the safest way to grow fruit was to pick it just as soon as it could be removed from the tree without damage. This was in part because during the middle of the nineteenth century, the Gold Rush was on and fresh fruit was exacting incredible prices in the mines. To reach the market, the fruit was shipped overland, so early harvest ensured it would not be overripe or susceptible to bruising and rot while in transit. For during that time, the roads to the mining camps were little more than rough trails, often hewn in nearly vertical cliffs. In some cases wagons could not pass, and pack mules became the primary mode of shipment.

One reason for the high demand for fresh fruit was the widespread difficulty with scurvy, a disease resulting from insufficient vitamin C in the diet. Placer miners were often so obsessive about finding gold that they completely ignored their diets, eating only when it was absolutely necessary. Scurvy caused tenderness and swelling of the gums, tooth loss, extreme pain in the joints, and a host of other maladies that eventually drove the miners off their claims in search of relief. It is reported that the symptoms abated very soon after the consumption of vitamin C; therefore, any foods that proved effective were costly and rare.

One of the most well-known orchardists of this era was General John Sutter, who owned Hock Farm in Sutter County on the banks of the Feather River. Sutter devised an ornamental arrangement of fruit trees and fruiting shrubs that he felt would present a more attractive means of orchard design. However, time proved this plan was not efficient for maintaining or harvesting the trees and was eventually abandoned.

California was fortunate that so many of the early settlers were accomplished farmers, and their fruit gardens served as testing grounds for the well-known fruit tree cultivars of the East. They proved that some varieties produced better in California; these were quickly grafted and budded into new stock, so that by 1860 there was an overabundance of fruit harvested. The orchards planted in less productive Eastern varieties were abandoned, and during the depression of 1860-61 peaches sold for only a penny a pound, while much of the crop rotted on neglected trees. This is partly attributed to the reduction of demand in the placer mines, which by the end of the 1860s were for the most part played out. Secondly, the silver mines of Nevada were drawing miners from the Mother Lode at a record rate, greatly reducing the demand for food in California.

THE DETAILS: PICKET FENCES
AND ORCHARDS

Everywhere the country garden style, created of necessity by the early pioneers, has captured the hearts of Americans. It has transcended the years to remain intact despite the decline of the agrarian lifestyle. Yet there seems to be a yearning to return to the land and abandon the congestion of urban life. For those unable to move to a rural area, various components of the country style garden are still possible in a city yard so that the slower pace of farm life is suggested amidst the hustle of lot and block housing.

Rustic Fencing

Fences in the rural landscape were barriers designed to keep animals either in or out. The farmer will design his fence in a way that conserves material and labor, but is strong enough to contain the animals. Larger animals, such as cattle and horses, require extensive corrals with more linear feet of fencing, but the fence itself need not be particularly dense. Chickens, goats, sheep, and other barnyard animals can slip through small openings in fences, so their enclosures must be very dense, with tightly spaced members.

Rail fences are primarily for horses and cattle. The most primitive material for rails are poles of pine, usually lodgepole, or any type of straight-growing young tree that does not readily decompose. Split rails are made from a single tree trunk split lengthwise into segments of the desired size. The best trees for split rail are redwood or cedar, due to their soft and straight-grained wood, which is long-lasting against the elements. These two woods are preferable for posts of any kind of fence where there is contact with the soil and rotting is more prevalent. Some types of pine and fir are also used for split rails.

Later on, milled lumber also came into use as farm fencing, the white split rail being the most common today. Whitewashing large amounts of fencing is a chore, so dark stains grew more popular for their improved ability to help preserve the wood. Today the old rustic rail fences are making a comeback, although they can be very expensive if purchased new. Some companies are prefabricating pressure-treated lodgepole pine fencing systems for easy installation. Other hardy souls fortunate enough to have a source of timber have gone back to laboriously splitting their own. In most cases this character fencing is used on a more visible portion of the site, while the remainder is fenced with woven wire and metal or wood posts.

Picket fences, once called paling fences, have changed little since the first settlers built them at Plymouth Colony. There they split wood into appropriate dimensions and pounded one end into the soil. The opposite ends were woven together or tied to a top crossbar for stability. The drawback to these fences is that the part in the soil rots away, although the speed of decomposition varies depending on wood type and soil moisture content. On California's north coast, redwood paling fences that enclose sheep pastures defy the aging process.

These rustic fences later yielded to woven wire fencing of various densities, with either steel T posts or wooden posts as support. But with the dooryard garden becoming the guest entry to the farmhouse, fences grew more refined. Milled lumber eventually replaced the hand-split pickets, the fences sometimes painted white or left to weather naturally. New methods of construction ensured that the expensive milled pickets no longer contacted the soil, thus becoming far more long-lasting. The front gate in the days of horse and buggy became a place to tether the horse. Arbors were spread over the gate to create a flower-laden gateway where the visitor could pause beneath the shade before entering the house.

The picket fence of the farm was a far cry from more elaborately decorated fences of the Victorians. True country-style pickets are simple, almost plain. Their arrangement, height, and spacing varied with what was available in that region at the time. But to the woman of the homestead, construction of a prim, front dooryard fence was the ultimate in rural refinement. Though the more utilitarian forms of paling fences still crisscrossed the barnyard, their purely functional purpose required no aesthetic improvement.

Outbuildings

A working farm of the nineteenth century was a collection of structures that included the house, barn, and various outbuildings. Even the most destitute homesite had an outhouse, the "necessary" located downwind and a short hike from the house. Some farms contained a root cellar, often built into a hillside, where the surrounding soil helped regulate the temperature year-round. A smokehouse, usually constructed of stone, provided a suitable means for preserving meat without drying or salting.

One of the most familiar sights in the California landscape is the water tower rising two or three stories above each farmhouse. It contained an elevated wood tank that was fully enclosed by walls and a roof. Water was pumped out of the well or other water source and boosted up into the tank. The gravity flow through a pipe originating at this height was sufficient to pressurize the household supply without electrically operated equipment. Some of the finest preserved water towers can be found in the town of Mendocino, standing well above the rooftops, each with slightly different design details. The particular reason for their longevity is the redwood they are built of, which was once plentiful in these north coast logging towns. Many are being turned into living quarters, with the elevated view in great demand. They also have been turned into shops, studios, and guest houses with rustic character difficult to create in contemporary buildings.

Agrarian Antiques

In most parts of California, obtaining water, the most essential yet irregular resource, was a chancy affair until deep, domestic wells were drilled. Functional windmill water pumps once were more numerous in our rural landscape, drawing water from the depths of the earth into either a domestic water tank or a stock trough. Many still whirl, but only a few function as pumps, the rest preserved as agrarian antiques.

One look at the equipment used by modern farmers, and it is understandable why so many old wagons and implements are now relegated to ornamental plantings. Far more of them are still sitting idle in remote agricultural communities of the central valley, although many wooden wagons and buggies are avidly collected whether functional or not.

An abandoned hay rake on the far corner of a field calls forth memories of our farming aesthetic. Its steel is now brown with rust, and the hawks perch on its members for a better view of prey, where there may be nothing taller on the fertile plain for miles. Lanky weeds stand amidst the tines, their heavy seed heads bending down with the breeze as if to taunt the once powerful tool now relegated to fallow ground. Perhaps there is no better mission than to rescue old farm equipment from the scrapyard. Icons of another era, they immediately bring to the garden a rural character, a reminder of our agrarian roots, when the soil and climate of California meant abundant life to those who came thousands of miles to share in the promise of Eden.

REDWOODS AND
GOLD DUST

ew states experienced such booming development as California did during the Victorian era, the period spanning the late 1840s to about 1900. California had earlier been little more than a sleepy outpost of Mexico, with an economy that relied heavily on its vast cattle ranches. With statehood, the land became available to Americans, and the natural resources were sought out and exploited during the latter half of the nineteenth century. This was also a period which saw the dawning of the industrial revolution, when American economic power grew steadily with the mechanization of manufacturing. It was also the time when railroads finally linked California with the rest of the United States and opened it up for easier immigration.

California's two greatest natural resources proved to be gold and timber, with these industries concentrated in the northern half of the state. Not until much later did oil drilling and development of massive irrigation projects stimulate growth in the south. Monterey was the capital during the Mexican era and for a while afterward, but San Francisco acted as the center for commerce and culture during the Victorian era.

Before the discovery of gold at Coloma, San Francisco was a small port called Yerba Buena on a nearly empty coastline. In just two years after the gold strike at Sutter's Mill, San Francisco became the main port for massive immigration by argonauts, those who chose a sea voyage to the goldfields. It also became the port for goods shipped by sea to supply the needs of the mining trade, along with the subsequent needs and whims of newly wealthy residents.

The gold-bearing areas of the Sierra were called the Mother Lode. It was a long, narrow strip varying from 1,000 to 3,000 feet in elevation and stretching from Sonora northward to Sierra City. Hundreds of camps were strung out along the corridor, and those on the main supply routes grew into sizeable towns. These were supplied by centers on the valley floor such as Stockton, Sacramento, and Marysville, all connected to San Francisco by a network of rivers and bays that allowed steamboats to move materials at low cost.

Gold tends to occur naturally in quartz veins in the Mother Lode. Millions of years of erosion, earthquakes, and volcanic activity

Governor's Mansion, Sacramento. (*Sacramento Museum of History*)

have crushed and broken up many of these veins, which were washed into the waterways during spring runoffs. Placer mining is a means of separating out this streambed alluvial gold from its surrounding gravels. Due to a heavy specific gravity, gold dust and fragments naturally sift down to the lowest levels of these gravel deposits, ultimately resting upon bedrock or very dense, ancient clay layers that hardened into cementlike aggregates. The process of placer mining was simply using moving water to separate gold from the surrounding gravels. Panning was most laborious, but sluice boxes sped up the process considerably.

There was a climate of euphoria in California during the 1850s, when it was expected that anyone who reached the goldfields could strike it rich overnight. The truth was that by 1860 much of the available placer gold was already extracted, and a vast majority of the miners were suffering the effects of their compulsive and often foolhardy attempts at mining. Life in the "diggins" was not easy: Miners often stood daily for months at a time in the ice-cold Sierra runoff, and the backbreaking labor of sifting through tons of gravel and the dilemmas of little food or medical care often left them weak, ill, or crippled. Some of the most visible legacies of these hordes of gold-seekers are the large cemeteries and the acres of wild Scotch broom (*Cytissus racemosus*) blanketing the countryside of the Mother Lode.

Gold that still lay encased in quartz underground was mined by hardrock tunneling. On the hilltops around Grass Valley in Nevada County, exposed quartz outcroppings bearing veins were discovered by prospectors. It was not until years later, though, that the hardrock mining process was improved enough to make ore extraction profitable. The largest of many hardrock operations was the Empire Mine, owned by the Bourn family of San Francisco, who also resided at Filoli, their country estate in Woodside. The Empire produced 5,800,000 *ounces* of gold out of a network of tunnels 367 miles long. This and the wealth produced by other hardrock mining ventures financed the legendary gambling halls, brothels, and lavish hotels of San Francisco's Barbary Coast.

Perhaps the most devastating facet of the mining industry was hydraulic mining, which was first developed in the North Bloomfield area outside Nevada City. The most ancient streambeds, laid down in the Tertiary period, were buried in gravel deposits beneath coverings of topsoil. These beds had been uplifted into dry hills, no longer serving as river courses.

They still contained large deposits of alluvial gold, however, and when standard placer mines played out, a new technique was developed to work these "dry diggins." A series of flumes and ditches were built to divert water from rivers much higher in the mountains, and the accumulated pressure at the lowest point was considerable. Large "monitors," or nozzles, were attached to the hoses, concentrating water into a hard stream that literally dissolved entire hillsides of these ancient gravels in just a matter of hours.

The monitors proceeded to destroy huge areas of countryside, and many of the scars can still be seen at Malakoff Diggins State Park. But the real damage occurred in our waterways, which provided drainage for the runoff from hydraulic mining. With the water came millions of cubic tons of "slickins," which clogged the channels and caused total destruction of mining claims downstream as well as devastation of riparian habitat.

Even today the Middle Fork of the Yuba River is still so choked with gravel that the water is hidden beneath the surface, which appears more like a dry streambed in the Mohave Desert. But what really caused the eventual outlawing of hydraulic mining was flooding in the valley and the covering of thousands of acres of prime farmland with gravel tailings. Even worse, trees, brush, and other organic material would act as a dam behind which the tailings would back up in the river canyons; the dams would later break under the pressure and send huge waves of water and mud churning down the narrow canyons of the Yuba, inundating all claims and camps in its path.

During this time the incredible wealth coming out of California made it feasible to consider laying track over the mighty Sierra to provide a more swift overland route. To build the railroad required armies of laborers, and those who had come for the Gold Rush demanded higher wages. Many, once hired, promptly abandoned the railroad for a second chance at fortune in the silver strikes of Nevada's Comstock Lode. This California labor problem was complicated by the Civil War, which reduced the number of new immigrants from the other states. As a result, highly controversial contracts were arranged to import Chinese laborers, who would work diligently for less demanding wages. These foreigners managed to lay track over the heights of the Sierra at Immigrant Gap and finally linked California with the rest of the civilized world at Promontory, Utah, in 1869.

Sutter's Mill was a lumber mill, part of an industry existing in California long before the Gold Rush population boom. But the

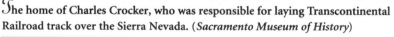

The home of Charles Crocker, who was responsible for laying Transcontinental Railroad track over the Sierra Nevada. (*Sacramento Museum of History*)

influx of resident miners stimulated the need for timber, as towns and cities sprang up throughout the north state. And it was inevitable that the great coast redwood trees (*Sequoia sempervirens*) of northwestern California were exploited for lightweight timber with remarkable resistance to decomposition. All along the north coast, small towns became ports for the shipping of timber to San Francisco and other points southward. A close relative, the big trees of the Sierra, *Sequoiadendron giganteum*, some of the largest known living things, were also logged, but with far less success than the coastal groves.

Southern California grew at a much slower rate than in the north, for it lacked both gold and timber. Perhaps more important was the fact that much of the Southland was without water in a climate of irregular and limited rainfall. The great fertile valleys of Los Angeles and its surrounding communities were of little use without water, but during the nineteenth century three factors influenced the subsequent explosion of growth in the south. Newly developed irrigation systems brought water to entire communities at once, such as to Ontario, rather than to just one ranch or mission site. Second, the railroad linked the north and south halves of the state, allowing health-seekers to immigrate or vacation comfortably in the temperate climate of Los Angeles. Third, the drilling and pumping of crude oil along the coast stimulated yet another economic boom of exploited natural resources.

During the Victorian era the accomplishments in the field of botany were many, and for the general population, horticulture became the rage, with the interest in plants and gardens never greater,

The Victorian era is perfectly expressed in this rural home, with heavily ornamented architecture, an elaborate front fence, and the combination of citrus and palms. (*Community Memorial Museum*)

A drawing of the Hazard home on Spring Street in Los Angeles, which portrays the ideals of Victorian gardens, including the assortment of trees, planted urns, statuary, and a heavily ornamented front fence. (*Thompson and West*, History of Los Angeles County)

particularly in newly wealthy California. The climate was mild enough to grow practically any plant, even exotic tropicals, on the south coast. Remember that the overwhelming majority of residents here, arriving during and after the Gold Rush, came from Eastern states. The winters of their previous homes could be so bitter only deciduous shrubs and conifers grew outdoors year-round. Imagine their delight at the myriad plants our climate could support, those with large, succulent leaves or odd, feathery forms. It is understandable that, like kids in a candy store, the Victorians used their new-found wealth to purchase the greatest diversity of plants possible for their homesites.

The gingerbread decoration of sometimes garish Victorian architecture became a visible sign of wealth, and the surrounding gardens also reflected this through a wide variety of plants. The Victorian garden was more of a botanical showcase than a well-designed out-door space, and the more exotic or rare the plants, the higher the social status of the resident. In California the use of subtropical plants, notably palm trees, became common, and to this day they are considered a hallmark of our state.

Perhaps most unique to this era was the practice of carpet bed-ding, which was displayed within the lawns of affluent residences and many of the larger resort hotels. Arranging various low-growing plants into precise patterns upon the ground mimicked Persian car-pets or other designs based upon geometric symmetry. Plants used for carpet bedding were either naturally compact in form or propagated to grow that way. Color for the pattern was derived from either flow-ers or foliage, plants with colored leaves being more reliable and capa-ble of supporting the design over a longer period. Fortunately, the practice died out, for it required daily tedious attention to keep the plantings manicured into the proper shapes and forms.

The Victorian era was considered a time of romantic notions set amidst rigid morals, and these two points of view were also manifest in gardens. While carpet bedding demanded a totally controlling hand, the romanticists leaned toward the softness of weeping foliage and rampant growth of vines to shroud homes and gazebos.

A newfound interest in natural history brought into fashion exotic plants gathered from the jungles of Asia, Africa, and South America. Botanical explorers shipped new plants to California that had been collected on expeditions to the far corners of the globe. Some chose not to leave California but to explore the less traveled parts of the state in search of native species. With the public clamoring for new plants, nurseries were hard-pressed to provide not only traditional garden plants but new ones as well. This was a time when the horti-culturists in the West shared their discoveries through various publi-cations, exchanging seeds and plants to improve the diversity of the nursery industry. Even today California remains a leader in retail land-scape plants because the climate is mild enough to easily propagate and grow plants without special protection during the winter.

Today we may thank the Victorian gardeners and the dedicated horticulturists of the day, who are responsible for a great number of plants we consider standard fare. To illustrate just how important this era was to the development of our state, it is estimated that eighty per-cent of the species cultivated today were first introduced in the peri-od from 1850 to 1900. Although Victorians' gardens tended to be as cluttered as their homes, and the practice of carpet bedding thankfully died out, it was this time of floramania and botanical fads that contributed most to the verdant reputation of our state.

THE FLORA OF THE VICTORIAN ERA

The Redwoods

The name *redwood* will always conjure up visions of massive trees rising hundreds of feet, their foliage disappearing into the clouds. No other tree, native or exotic, can compare with its graceful beauty, sheer size, and commercial productivity. Redwood is the common name for two species, both native to California. There is always confusion as to which redwood is which. *Sequoiadendron giganteum* is the Sierra redwood, or big tree, which grows inland, and only on the western slopes of the Sierra Nevada. It is more massive, but not as tall as its coastal cousin, *Sequoia sempervirens*. The coast redwood thrives only in the coastal mountain ranges of the north half of the state. A moisture-loving species, it is by far the taller but tends to be thinner than the inland redwood species. Although both redwood trees are native, the coast redwood can also be found in Oregon. Redwood trees played important parts in the material culture of many Native Californian tribes, but these trees became famous worldwide only during the latter half of the nineteenth century.

Coast Redwood
Sequoia sempervirens

Along the northern coast,
Just back from the rock-bound shore and the caves,
In the saline air from the sea in the Mendocino country,
With the surge for bass and accompaniment low and hoarse,
With crackling blows of axes sounding musically driven
    by strong arms,
Riven deep by the sharp tongues of the axes, there in the
    redwood forest dense,
I heard the mighty tree its death-chant chanting. . . .

WALT WHITMAN
From "Song of the Redwood-Tree"

*S*equoiadendron giganteum in the Sierra Nevada. (*California State Library*)

There are few places as mysterious and awe inspiring as an old-growth redwood glade. There is little sound except the wind moaning in the dense canopy above. Few plants, save some ferns and mosses, live on the forest floor, which is carpeted in a thick litter of redwood leaves and cones. Yet, even a good-sized second-growth forest is nearly as awesome, for the trees reach incredible heights after just fifty to seventy-five years.

The coast redwood was a valuable source of wood to the numerous tribes which lived on the northwestern coasts. A tree was felled by building fires around the base, which gradually ate into the trunk until the tree toppled over. The tribes, which relied heavily on fishing for their food, used deep boats carved from redwood tree trunks to travel by water up and down the coastline and ply the larger rivers. Their houses, squarish gabled cabins, were constructed with redwood slabs split into planks by elk antler wedges. Mussel shells sufficed for carving tools, and some artisans carved artifacts that survived only because of the durability of the wood.

When Fra Junipero Serra, the founder of our mission chain, was preparing to die, he asked that his coffin be made of redwood trees from the vicinity of Carmel. In it he was buried at Mission San Carlos Borromeo in 1784. Nearly one hundred years later, the redwood coffin of the padre was accidently rediscovered fully intact during excavations on mission grounds, proving the longevity of the wood is not just legend. Another testament is Fort Ross just north of Bodega Bay, built in 1812 and still standing today.

During the Gold Rush and the sudden rise in population that followed, building materials were in great demand. Early photos of Nevada City show the surrounding hills virtually barren, as all the timber had been used for either shoring, flumes, buildings, or firewood. One unique quality of redwood is its low resin content, which makes it highly absorbent of water. This proved invaluable for building flumes, which supplied both the dry diggins and various irrigation needs. There are even reports of redwood blackboards made of single slabs four feet square and even larger. Here and in less timbered parts of the Mother Lode, lumber was such an important commodity, it sold at incredible prices.

At the Empire Mine State Park is a good example of this demand for redwood in building. The Bourn cottage was built on the mine site in 1898, and the entire first floor is paneled in old-growth heart redwood. The boards are without flaw and remain untreated to this day. The wood is so porous, visitors are asked to avoid touching it because oil from the hand is rapidly drawn into the wood and results in immediate discoloration. Throughout much of northern California, redwood was carved and turned into some of the most elaborate decorative pieces found anywhere in Victorian architecture.

Redwood casks are known to impart no flavoring into their contents. Early California vintners discovered this and constructed enormous tanks of redwood, which would absorb liquid and swell to create a very tight seal for long-term storage of aging wine. Today many of these old tanks are proving excellent for water storage despite their advanced age.

As anyone familiar with the north coast knows, the roads to the redwood forest are still nearly as torturous as they were in the 1800s. Lumber markets at that time were in San Francisco, and the best transportation was by ship. The timber industry was responsible for many of our most picturesque towns of Mendocino County, isolated Victorian villages that were virtually abandoned with the decline of the great forests. In 1850 the population of the logging town of Eureka numbered over three thousand. At the town of Mendocino the enterprising Chinese used the flow of tides to drive a Muley perpendicular saw.

To many the heyday of redwood logging of the north coast was similar to that of the Gold Rush. Faced with the largest trees they had ever seen, loggers were hard-pressed to drag their fallen trunks with yokes of oxen to the mills. A young blacksmith, John Dolbeer, invented a steam winch to hoist the trees far more quickly, hastening the destruction of the forests. At its peak, larger mills were putting out 600,000 board feet of finished lumber per day.

Timber regulation came into being as conservationists sought to reduce the incredible rate of destruction. In 1917 the Save-the-Redwoods League was formed, and it is still active today, buying land to add acreage to their preservation zones.

Coast redwoods love moisture and require the heavy rainfall of the northern coast to reach their ultimate size and health. Those which naturally occur south of San Francisco, where it's drier, never reach the same proportions. The trees are considered the tallest in the world, although some Australian eucalyptus are now known to rival this claim. A coast redwood tree can be expected to live from 1,000 to 1,500 years, a shorter life span that its interior cousin, the big tree.

There are now many cultivars of *Sequoia sempervirens* widely used in landscaping. The problem is that the trees are often "limbed up" from their base to expose the trunk and soil beneath the dripline. In their natural environment, trees grow close together and their roots are always shaded and well mulched with a litter of leaves, stems, and cones. When the trees are limbed up, the roots heat up, more moisture evaporates from the soil surface, and the trees tend to sucker heavily from the burly base of the trunk in an effort to shade the root zone. Redwood trees are not naturally suited for inland heat. Be kind to young redwoods by planting them closer together, and leave their trunks swathed in boughs. Provide plenty of water to help compensate for the heat, and the little trees will return the favor by growing much faster. They will also take on the rich green of coastal trees, while those less pampered can be easily picked out of town scenes by their browner leaf tips.

Giant Sequoia, Big Tree
Sequoiadendron giganteum

I feel most emphatically that we should not turn into shingles a tree which was old when the first Egyptian conqueror penetrated to the valley of the Euphrates.
PRESIDENT THEODORE ROOSEVELT
after visiting sequoia groves with John Muir, 1903

The giant sequoia is a drought-resistant tree thriving at higher elevations of the Sierra, between 4,500 and 8,000 feet. They are quite at home with annual snowfalls to ten feet followed by incredibly dry summers. One interesting feature of the trees is they tend to appear in groves which today are named and have become popular tourist sites in protected National Forests. The trees were first named *Wellingtonia gigantia* in honor of Arthur Welleseley, Duke of Wellington, a hero of the Battle of Waterloo. After much controversy, the genus name was changed to *Sequoia* to commemorate the Cherokee leader, Sequoyah (1770–1843), who devised the eighty-three-character Cherokee alphabet. The wood of the giant sequoia is highly resistant to decomposition, and much of the research on size and longevity is done by studying dead trees which have lain in the same place for thousands of years.

One factor which has assisted their longevity is the unique spongy bark, which acts much the same way as asbestos when exposed to fire. On large specimens this insulating bark may be up to two feet thick. Small saplings that have not yet developed this fire-proof bark are vulnerable to wildfires, but fires can sweep through the Sierra and never damage sufficiently mature redwoods. Once sheep began to graze in the Sierra, shepherds set frequent fires to thin out the underbrush and encourage more grass. These fires were more frequent than would naturally occur in the area, as a result interrupting the regeneration of sequoias by burning out seedlings in consecutive years.

The discovery of big tree groves occurred in 1852, while the California Gold Rush was in full swing. A.T. Dowd, a hunter for the Union Water Company, came into a grove while chasing a bear. He

Sequoiadendron giganteum at Sequoia National Park. Depicted are two of the largest, named General Grant and General Sherman. (*California State Library*)

$\mathcal{A}$ close look at this old lithograph of the Mammoth Tree Grove in Calaveras County reveals how they were viewed by citizens of the time. The bark of this majestic old tree has been stripped off, which killed it a short time after. The bark was removed to be transported and reassembled as an exhibit in the eastern United States and Europe to prove such massive trees indeed existed. The caption describes it as "500,000 feet of inch lumber," a sorry epitaph for such a beautiful and ancient monument.

was so astounded by the massive trees, he immediately returned to camp with news of the discovery. The next interested party was botanist Dr. Albert Kellogg, who traveled to the Calaveras Grove to take specimens of the trees. From his glowing reports the big trees became a botanical rage in England, and there developed a great demand for seed.

At the same time, big trees were viewed as a critical source of lumber for the furious mining in the Mother Lode. Redwood was valuable for flumes and sluices because it could remain in contact indefinitely with water and still resist rotting. The disadvantages of redwood is its lack of strength and brittle nature, making it poor material for structural beams and heavy-load timbers. Loggers invaded the redwood groves and began to topple the giants, only to find they literally shattered into pieces when they fell to the earth. As a result, the big trees were milled primarily into fence posts, grape stakes, and shingles, with only a small percentage of the wood suitable for the types of lumber yielded from coast redwood.

The limitations of big tree redwood did not stop logging, and there were ongoing legal battles as to who owned the trees and the land they stood upon. Disputes between conservationists, such as John Muir, and the numerous logging and grazing interests in the Sierra lasted for decades. Muir actually wrote letters using for ink the rosy purple drops of sequoia sap. In the letters he described the spiritual place of the trees in the lore of local Indian tribes. He reported the men drank the sap in belief that it granted mystical power, a practice no doubt born of awe at the giant trees. Finally, through widespread public interest, the Sequoia and General Grant national parks were founded to protect the trees. Still, illegal logging continued until John Muir demanded cavalry patrols be assigned to protect the trees. Eventually other parks were established to include outlying groves, so both Kings Canyon and Yosemite national parks ensure the big trees are preserved for generations to come.

Sequoiadendron giganteum is an excellent tree for drought-conscious landscapes, but it is not nearly as available or adaptable as the coast redwood. This is due to the limited natural range of the giant trees, which lies above 4,500 feet, and their requiring both winter cold and extreme dry summer heat to grow best. But where conditions are similar, this is an evergreen tree which may be planted and promptly forgotten. Its form is more rounded than the coast redwood's, with a softer overall appearance.

Legacies of the Irish and the Chinese

On Highway 49 just north of Nevada City is the tiny mining town of North San Juan. Travelers are notified of its impending presence by a noticeable change in vegetation. Gone are the manzanita, black oaks, and California lilac. Instead, the roadsides are crowded with dense thickets of broom and above it the tree-of-heaven. Neither are native to California, yet both overwhelmingly invasive species have displaced myriad botanical life forms.

Tree-of-heaven
Ailanthus altissima

The deciduous tree-of-heaven looks much the same as eastern sumacs and the black walnut, with long stems of pinnate leaves. Attractive, brick-red keys, or seed clusters, are similar to those of the ash and occur in autumn. The tree sprouts readily from seed. Chinese immigrants working in the gold camps frequently carried seed of this, their "temple tree," from their homeland. It grew so fast, putting on twenty feet of growth per year, and attained such large proportions, up to 100 feet, that the Chinese considered it capable of reaching the heavens. In California its Latin genus name was derived from the root word *ailanto*, which also means tall enough to reach the sky.

Another factor which may have increased its intrinsic value to the Chinese was the fact that *Ailanthus* foliage, like that of the mulberry, could be used to feed silkworms. They also knew the leaves actually produced a stronger and more durable silk fiber. There is some evidence that garments of fabric made of ailanthus silk could be worn through several generations of constant use. Due to the incredibly fast growth rate of these trees, silk could be produced for a quarter of the cost of traditional silk.

Tree-of-heaven is the consummate tree for the drought-tolerant garden. It grows in the worst soils, under our often scant rainfall, and suckers into unbelievably dense groves. These vigorous qualities have their drawbacks, for although they manage to survive in these inhospitable Sierra foothills, they are unruly and invasive. So tenacious is the plant that huge specimens can be found growing out of tiny slots in pavement or building foundations. It is a wonder the constricted vascular cambium can transport sufficient water to stimulate such incredible top growth.

A big problem with *Ailanthus* is the male flowers, which emit a potent and unpleasant odor. Dense groves that envelop older home-sites practically drive the residents from their houses during the blooming season. When naturally reproducing groves occur, plants are extremely prolific and there is no control over the numbers of male plants. A single adult may also reproduce extensively by sucker-ing. Fortunately, one can be assured a female plant from growers, who propagate by root cuttings of the desired sex.

There is much controversy over the tree-of-heaven invasions of the gold country of the Sierra and other rural areas of California and the West. It was first introduced to England in 1751, then came to the New World, where it was a popular street tree for a while. In California's perpetually marshy, tule-choked Central Valley, malaria did occur, as it did in many American towns. Due to the tree-of-heaven's ability to thrive despite the filth and smoke of large cities, it was thought the trees acted like a filter to remove smoke and malari-al poisons, which at that time were not yet attributed to mosquitoes. This factor led to more widespread planting of the trees. But when epidemics proved the trees didn't stop malaria, public opinion swayed to believe that the odors of the male flowers were actually due to the trees' releasing of toxins they had accumulated, so most of the trees were promptly cut down.

Scotch Broom
Cytisus scoparius

The great drifts of yellow-gold blossoms that appear in tandem with the orchid of native western redbud represent another of our love-hate relationships with exotic plants. The Scotch broom was bequeathed to us by tin miners from Cornwall, England, who came to California in droves to work in the world-famous hardrock quartz mines of Grass Valley. There are many other related shrubs called broom, but few are as prolific in their seed-bearing as this one.

Like the Chinese, the miners valued their plant as a symbol of their homeland. There broom provided fodder for sheep and valuable heat-ing fuel in the nearly treeless Scotland. Like the sagebrush that is so typ-ical of the dry Western landscape, the broom groves of Britain inhabit-ed the most infertile hillsides, becoming popular places for lovers to meet unobserved. And in spring the bright flowers also emitted a pleas-ant fragrance, which led to one of its common names, sweet broom.

Broom, as befits its name, was bundled into brushes and brooms of many sizes, some used green to sweep out hot brick baking ovens, due to their natural fire-resistant properties. Its seeds were pickled and substituted for capers. The foliage has been used for thatching, as pulp for paper or cloth, as well as in the tanning process. Broom is an ancient medicinal and was so effective for liver and kidney ailments, it was put to use as recently as World War II.

In North San Juan and points northward to Downieville and south beyond Grass Valley, botanists are concerned over the potential displacement of native plants. In fact, broom has invaded natural ecosystems throughout the Pacific Northwest. The shrubs grow so densely, there is no light to support seedlings of trees, so when existing trees eventually die, there are no others to take their places. The result is large expanses of nothing but broom, and there is no way to check its spreading. A Christmas tree farmer outside North San Juan laments that the broom is her chief weed, persistently invading her stand of conifers. As a shrub, it is far more difficult to control or—heaven forbid—kill with herbicide. For all rural gardeners, it is unwise to plant broom. Even though some types are not so invasive, it can be impossible for the novice to know one variety from the other before it is too late.

The Eucalypts

No other tree has changed the face of the California countryside as completely as the eucalyptus (*Eucalyptus* spp.). It blankets the hills in groves, borders orchards as tightly spaced windrows, and occasionally a lone specimen can be found, like a timeless sentinel, marking the site of a forgotten rancher's homesite. Imagine a California without these trees, no trace of the familiar pungent scent, floating upon the warm breezes of a summer dusk or growing potent with the first rains of autumn. And in the parched heat of our inland valleys, there would be but little shade without their weeping limbs, with their dangling leaves of turquoise and jade. How sad it would be if no children had ever delighted in stripping great sheets of curling bark from the buff-toned trunks, then crushing them loudly to pieces in their little hands.

The eucalypts are Australian natives and constitute much of the forest in that far-off continent. Over four hundred different species are recorded, but only about fifteen are used in Western landscaping

$\mathcal{A}$ mature eucalyptus windrow in the dry southern California countryside while horse and wagon was still the most common mode of transportation. (*California State Library*)

today. Residents of California during the nineteenth century were faced with an arid climate where very few of their favorite Eastern forest trees would thrive on the scant rainfall, warm winter, and extremely long summer. It is understandable that when San Francisco nurseryman William C. Walker first announced his procurement of *Eucalyptus globulus*, a new drought-resistant tree which promised an incredible growth rate, Californians must have clamored for it. But not until 1863 did the first sizable supply arrive. These were divided among owners of some of the largest ranchos for testing. The ranches included Verdugo, Workman, Banning, Sanchez, and Wolfskill, which would later boast the largest single specimen in the state.

It was not long before the reputation of the eucalyptus tree reached outlying areas, and a tremendous demand grew for seedlings. The new tree for California could be planted to line driveways, as a windbreak, or simply as a reliable, fast-growing source of shade, most welcome on hot inland homesites. Eucalyptus is difficult if not impossible to propagate by cuttings, but it will sprout within days from seed. This is the reason why there can be such diversity within a single species of eucalyptus, for each seed contains slightly different genetic material. Planting from seed is fast and easy for the nursery-man, and it has been proven that the sooner the seedling is transplanted out of its pot into garden soil, the faster it will ultimately grow.

When the many species of eucalyptus came pouring into California, speculators began to envision great forests which could quickly mature into marketable lumber. The railroad saw the trees as a ready supply of fuel and planted blocks along their rail lines. During the Victorian era there was interest in "gumwood" furniture, which was made from eucalyptus trees. Great stands of eucalyptus were planted throughout the state, which were to harvest high profit margins for their owners.

But when the first were to be logged, there arose a number of unexpected problems. To begin with, as mentioned above, there was a great deal of variation within a species, rendering many of the trunks unsuitable for different reasons. The fastest growing trees proved to have hollow or rotten cores of heartwood. In many, the sapwood dried at a considerably faster rate than the heartwood, causing the logs to check and crack. If the logs were felled and not cut immediately, the soft wood quickly hardened and became difficult to mill. Many of the species planted by the railroad proved unsuitable even for firewood; as a result, these eucalyptus plantations were abandoned to survive entirely on their own.

Although abandoned by speculators, these early groves became the sources of tree seed for local farms and ranches. After the first groves had been logged, they were found to stump-sprout into clean, straight poles, which became popular for fence posts and rails. This practice is still actively used today in southern Africa, where great plantations of these trees are cut at regular intervals for poles. Straight and plentiful, they are used in Third World countries for just about anything from rafters to fence posts.

California's eucalyptus windrows have become landmarks, often remaining long after the citrus or avocado groves they protected had been removed for development. The greatest advantage of eucalyptus is its disease resistance; for the time invested in developing

Winter at the cattle ranch.

Marshland sprouting dense tules and cattails were common in the lowlands of the Central Valley.

A very old lilac in the yard of a miner's cabin in the Mother Lode.

A lilac in a miner's cabin yard.

Very old cottonwood on an abandoned farm site in the Sacramento Valley.

Cottonwood trees in full autumn color.

$\mathcal{P}$ink oleander flowers.

$\mathcal{T}$he segmented fertile stems of horsetails.

$\mathcal{T}$he red fence rose grew popular with the variety 'Paul's Scarlet', which grew vigorously and bloomed repeatedly. Widely propagated, it became a favorite throughout the West. Later on, it was improved by breeding into 'Blaze', the variety of red fence rose most widely planted today.

𝒜 red rose arbor in an old graveyard. Old roses could survive longterm neglect and the dry conditions of early communities, when water was still drawn by hand from the well.

𝒜 blooming almond orchard and pasture beyond.

An old apple tree still producing after half a century. Many of the old fruit trees found today have grown from old rootstocks, which are unusually hardy compared to the varieties often grafted onto them.

Though this farmhouse was abandoned long ago, a single apple tree remains to bloom in a snow of white every spring. Living on ground water, it alone survived while the rest of the small orchard died out. The oleander, another tenacious survivor, will bloom in blood red flowers later in the year.

Fencing in redwood country was designed to enclose sheep and thus had to be tightly spaced. Decomposition-resistant redwood pickets could be pounded into the soil and connected by only a single top rail.

A "Virginia fence" of split redwood.

An old redwood water tower with tank.

$\mathcal{I}$nspired by the historic water towers of rural California, this new structure has an open sun deck and provides a view over the treetops.

$\mathcal{W}$estern artifacts like this old buckboard are charming, rustic additions to our gardens, but they are growing scarce. (*California Department of Water Resources*)

$\mathcal{T}$his unique gate was designed and built by Susan Elmore to incorporate pieces of rusted wagon iron she dug up at an old farm. Alone, each piece is not particularly noteworthy, but together they are a tribute to the past.

Above: A modern example of carpet bedding.

Left: The Bourn Cottage at the Empire Mine, California's largest hardrock gold mine. The cottage was built of overburden rock hauled from the mine shafts, thus making it an intrinsic part of the Mother Lode.

Second-growth *Sequoia sempervirens* surrounding a burned-out stump well over a hundred years old. Most of the old growth was logged off in the nineteenth century and the slash burned.

Tree-of-heaven in Nevada City laden with brown seedpods at the end of the season.

Scotch broom growing strictly on natural rainfall. Soon this pasture will be inundated with seedlings.

$\mathcal{A}$ forest of eucalyptus seedlings sprung up amidst an old Victorian graveyard. The ground is littered with sheets of bark, which have peeled off the trunks and branches high above.

$\mathcal{T}$he old farmhouse and camellia bush hidden behind a windbreak of eucalyptus and cypress.

$\mathcal{O}$ne of the few blooms that appear on the ancient camellia.

Camellia shrubs were favorites of the Victorian gardener and can be found in many old gardens.

A windmill palm at 2,000 feet above sea level in the Sierra. An even older specimen can be seen in Nevada City, an additional 3,000 feet higher. This proves these slow-growing, rugged little palms withstand incredibly low temperatures, heavy snows, and very arid conditions.

Smaller landscape palms, such as these Mediterranean fan palms and pygmy date palms, fit well into the foundation planting of Victorian and, in this case, arts-and-crafts-style homes.

A unique combination, but so typically southern Californian, of rampantly growing climbing roses and palms.

An old specimen of *Chamerops humilis*, the Mediterranean fan palm, which is still in demand for its small size and unusual clumping habit.

$\mathcal{D}$ragon's blood dracaena.

$\mathcal{T}$ower-of-jewels.

$\mathcal{M}$ost people attempted to make their milled picket fences as elaborate as possible.

Cast iron fences were used by row house owners to enclose their basement entries.

Old gates or segments of iron fencing make perfect garden accents. Taller gates have been made by standing spans of iron fencing on end.

Above: A contemporary yet traditional gazebo uses lath as roofing material. Although it doesn't provide shelter from the rain, the open top keeps the gazebo cooler by allowing air to rise out.

Left: This small garden house was once a pit privy (outhouse). With the advent of indoor plumbing, it was remodeled into a shed.

$\mathcal{R}$uins of miner's cabins, rock walls, old stone foundations, and newly constructed rock walls are all valuable in the landscape. When the stone is obtained locally, especially on-site, it is better integrated into the whole. On old sites where blackberry or vinca vines have shrouded these artifacts, the vegetation should be removed so we might better appreciate the sense of history.

$\mathcal{A}$ ram's head urn is highly decorative and could serve as both statuary and plant container.

$\mathcal{W}$ith the advent of water towers and wind-driven pumps, old wells were either abandoned or capped off with mechanical devices. Those which did remain as decorative elements in gardens are a lingering vestige of frontier life.

a windbreak, this feature was most important. Farmers found the eucalyptus lacked enough lower foliage and so devised a two-species windbreak. On the coast it was a combination of Monterey cypress (*Cupressus macrocarpa*) and eucalyptus, usually *Eucalyptus globulus*. Inland the combination was eucalyptus and California pepper (*Schinus molle*), which was no doubt an attractive combination. The old trees still living have become dangerous in high winds, for their aboveground mass has grown far too large for their root systems to support under the wind load. In many cases, hardpan soils have stimulated a pancaked root system, very shallow and without the taproot for stability.

To the untrained eye, and even to some half-trained eyes, all eucalyptus species look the same. The most distinctive difference is in the bark, which is grouped into three types. The bloodwoods have rough, short-fibered bark cracked into rectangular scales. An example is *Eucalyptus citriodora*, or lemon-scented gum. Ironbarks have just that, a very hard, deeply furrowed bark, typically in dark colors, as in *Eucalyptus sideroxylon* 'Rosea', or pink ironbark. Gums, making up the largest group, exhibit the soft, buff tones of typical eucalyptus bark, which peels away in stiff sheets every few years, as with *Eucalyptus grandis*, rose gum.

Eucalypts are notorious for their litter of bark, seedpods, and leaves. Old blocks of tightly spaced trees are virtually carpeted in the stuff, making a terrible fire hazard. Eucalyptus leaves are the source of a medicinal oil, widely used in bronchial remedies and in the past considered an antiseptic. The presence of this oil in eucalyptus litter acts to discourage understory plants that might compete for moisture with the trees. It is rare to find any plants of size thriving within the dripline of eucalyptus trees except for grasses.

Some species of eucalyptus served another purpose. Malaria afflicted residents of lowland "fever districts" across the globe. Through a French experiment in Algeria, it was discovered that the eucalyptus trees were so drought-tolerant they literally sucked moisture out of the soil at an astounding rate to support their explosive top growth. If enough trees were planted, boggy wetlands could be dried up, and the threat of malaria was virtually eliminated. This same rampant growth afflicts eucalyptus with weak branches in cultivated landscapes where ground water, irrigation, or surface flows provide sufficient moisture. The trees should be pruned on a regular basis to avoid this weakness typical of many species. It is not uncom-

The Second Great Eucalyptus Boom-doggle

A second boom in commercial eucalyptus tree planting began in 1904, after a rumor that the United States was about to experience a crisis in availability of hardwood for building. Unfortunately, human memory is unusually short, and much of the earlier, albeit inaccurate, literature on the potential for milling eucalyptus was resurrected. By 1912 over 50,000 acres of eucalyptus trees were under cultivation in southern California. The turn-of-the-century influx of new residents into the now-irrigated Southland had also stimulated a high demand for eucalyptus trees for yard and garden.

It was considered a good risk to become a eucalyptus tree farmer because the demand was so great. However, the advertisements claiming eucalypts were carefree and drought-proof enough for even the most ignorant gardener were widely believed. But like all species, eucalyptus does have its limitations. Plantations located in very poor soils, cold mountains, and drought-prone communities of the Mohave failed, and many of these entrepreneurs went bankrupt as their trees promptly died.

Theodore Payne, an enterprising nurseryman in Los Angeles, maintained a more conservative view toward exploiting the demand. He began roaming the countryside to find the old groves of the 1860s in order to collect the seed; in one season he managed to gobble up over 1,500 pounds of various species' seeds. He began shipping everywhere that the climate was mild enough for the tree to survive, from South America to Europe.

Southern California continued to grow, and the eucalyptus reached its zenith of popularity about the time of the first World War. The war, and later the Great Depression, reduced the interest in trees and civic pride of the post-Victorian era. Not until the post-World War II building boom did demand for trees and landscape plants again surge in suburban southern California.

mon to find sizable fallen limbs beneath old stands of trees after windy weather. The perpetual topping not only strengthens the branching structure but encourages the root system to be more adventurous.

Unfortunately, many people underestimate the ultimate proportions of eucalyptus trees, which in their natural habitat are said to equal, and possibly surpass, the height of our coast redwoods. Eventually the trees must be cut down, for the once-gangling sapling may have taken over half the yard in its endless drive to produce yet more growth.

Camellia
Camellia japonica

On the north coast of Mendocino County is the sleepy little town of Manchester. Nestled amidst a windbreak of cypress and eucalyptus stands a farmhouse, now dilapidated and mildewed in the damp ocean air. It is built of very wide, handsawn heart redwood boards, the inside papered first in scraps of cotton dress cloth, then newspaper, and finally Victorian wallpaper, no doubt added later, when the rancher was more established. But what is most interesting about the site are two gnarled camellias, their twisted branches patterned in lichen and moss. They struggle amidst a sea of vinca that has blanketed the entire homestead nearly a foot and a half thick in foliage.

There in the weak light beneath the massive canopies, one of the camellias still blooms, its vibrant red blossoms seeming out of place in the moody dell of moss and shade. My friend Jim Thompson has generously shared this special place with me, and it sits quietly behind his own garden on a portion of the old homestead. He laments he could not convince the owner to sell him the house as well.

His practiced eye has studied the enigma of these camellias to assess their age and possible variety. It was he who first suggested the camellias of early California had originally come on the Manila galleons that sailed across the Pacific from the Orient to supply the isolated missions and ranchos here. We both marveled at the thought that these might be the original species, a true remnant of the Old West here on the coast.

Upon further study, I have come to believe he is right. The

camellia is named after Father George Joseph Kamel, a seventeenth-century Moravian Jesuit priest who made his life's work to serve in the Spanish missions of the Philippines. There, astounded by the beauty of the wild plants in those moist jungles, he collected many specimens on the island of Luzon and also found plants of interest in the door-yard gardens of Chinese and Japanese residents. He prepared numerous, detailed botanical drawings of these plants, which he sent back home to Spain. When he retired from active work, he sailed into a port of call in China, where he found camellias in bloom. Kamel collected seeds and cuttings and even brought to Europe a small potted plant for the emperor's wife, Maria Theresa. But Kamel grew homesick for the islands and soon returned to the Philippines, where he later died.

The fact that camellias were already under cultivation in Philippine gardens at the time of Kamel and that Manila galleons supplied the California missions suggests that camellia plants were likely to have been shipped there. It is possible that these flowers reached the California coast long before they were ever grown successfully in England or the east coast of the United States. We know the rancheros of the hide and tallow trade spent their money on fine fabrics and jewelry, even musk roses. It is not unreasonable to think the traders might also have brought seed, or even a potted camellia plant. Since camellias root easily from cuttings but require up to two years to germinate from seed, it is possible that a few individuals could have produced many identical daughter plants through vegetative propagation. Camellias take so perfectly to the northern California climate that it stands to reason that plants could have been widely distributed well before the Gold Rush.

From Kamel's gifts to the emperor's wife came many other camellias, joined by those discovered later, in the nineteenth century, when the botanical world was lusting for new and more exotic varieties. Sacramento, California, the thriving center of the Gold Rush is today deemed the camellia capital of the world, with plants blooming in February all over the city. Victorian homes downtown are banked with very old, tree-sized camellias that flower lustily and prove nearly as garish as the gingerbread architecture. A sizable grove of camellias was planted in Capitol Park, which surrounds the Sacramento Capitol, and another old grouping blooms each year in front of the Hall of Records in Yuba City. Both are fine examples of how

Victorians combined colorful flowers with palm trees for a unique style of enhancing civic buildings.

While all these camellias are showing off in the valley, that scrubby, chlorotic plant at the farmhouse in Mendocino continues to haunt me. It attests to the true value of a camellia, which is so rugged it continues to bloom year after year despite the encroaching shade and greedy vinca. No hybrid could ever hold up under such neglect. I wonder where it really came from—perhaps a cutting of a plant once grown at Mariano Vallejo's rancho or at Mission San Raphael?

Ornamental Palms

A study of old photos of California's great Victorian mansions reveals frontyards that resemble botanical gardens. Extensive lawns were broken by single specimens of different types of trees. One might be a redwood, then beside it a southern magnolia, and a citrus ten feet away, and so on, filling the entire lawn at similar spacings. Without fail, there were always palms of various sorts interspersed with these more traditional trees. During the Victorian period in California, the torrid love affair with palms was at the first of its many peaks, usually followed by times when the trees were considered garish and in very poor taste. One example is the recent extensive planting of mature palms during the 1980s, but this current fad is waning, and soon the lucrative market for palms will disintegrate.

But to Victorians who grew up in the East, where plant selection was limited, the ability to grow something as unusual as a palm was considered the height of fashion. The wealthier the homeowner, the more diverse his or her palm collection would be. The demand for new and unusual palms was great during these years, especially for species that could survive mild frosts.

The railroad opened up southern California, where the warm, dry climate drew those suffering from chronic illnesses, primarily tuberculosis and other lung maladies. Many elaborate resorts were in demand to lodge these health-seekers. The most well known is the Hotel Del Coronado in San Diego, its landscaping by palm enthusiast Kate Sessions, who was also responsible for obtaining and propagating many of the commonly found species in favor today. All along the west coast, other resort hotels, such as the Del Monte, were being built in the high Victorian style, with extensive gardens of palms and exotics.

Only one species of palm is native to California. All others had to be discovered, brought to the West Coast, and then propagated for sale. The many nursery establishments that cropped up to feed the Victorian demand for exotics increased our knowledge of how palms function as plants. It was then that the portability of the palm was realized: Unlike most other trees, it can be transplanted even when very large, mature, and with only a small rootball.

This and other factors, such as their frost-tolerance, led to palms' distribution across the state into unlikely areas. A few years ago we had "big snow" here in Dobbins; while driving down a familiar road, the silhouette of a palm was clearly visible beneath a thick blanket of white. I had not noticed it before in the dense native vegetation, but since that day I have watched that old man of a palm for its incredible tolerance of extremes.

This one is *Trachycarpus fortunei*, the very slow-growing, dainty windmill palm, and since that snowy day I've discovered two more growing in the nearby Keystone Cemetery. The first palm was standing at the site of an old ranch, where during the summer it receives no water at all, and for decades of winters it has taken the worst conditions of the mighty Sierra. Someone who no doubt lived during Victorian times planted these trees as seedlings, for who else would think of planting palms in the pine forests of these mountains?

In southern California the palm boom really took off. The early development of Beverly Hills had the roadways flanked with tall-growing palms, including the familiar fan palms, Canary Island date palms, and queen palms, now also hallmarks of old San Diego. On a smaller scale, *Phoenix reclinata* became a foundation plant, windmill palms single specimens, and the Mediterranean fan palm, with its multiple trunks, an exotic of the highest order.

These palms of Victorian California were purely ornamental and often status symbols. They were not part of our material culture, as was the native desert fan palm. There was no need for fruit or symbolic fronds, as in the mission era, and landmarks were not important in nineteenth-century urban or suburban neighborhoods. But the roles of these trees throughout virtually every era in California, including the twentieth century, prove they are the epitome of our aesthetic. Though their popularity rises and falls with each generation, their adaptability and profound impact on landscape design will always keep them at home here on the balmy west coast.

Black Locust
Robinia pseudoacacia

The main street of the Mother Lode hamlet of Downieville is lined with very old black locust trees. They tower overhead to shade the town which is perched on the banks of the Downie and Yuba rivers. I believe this is by far the most beautiful of the still-living Gold Rush towns, partly due to the rivers but mostly because of the trees. Angels Camp, Sonora, Auburn, and even Nevada City can all bake beneath the California summer sun, for they are not blessed with such shade. These locusts are not native trees of the West, but were planted by miners with forethought and a strong sense of civic pride.

The black locust is a member of the legume clan, that group with pealike flowers, pods, and the unique ability to fix, or transfer, atmospheric nitrogen into the soil around their roots. The trees are laden in spring with chains of blooms, older varieties in white and some of the newer strains in orchid blooms resembling those of wisteria. They are also extremely drought-resistant plants, so much so that they have naturalized in many parts of California, much to the botanist's chagrin. They sprout so easily from seed, require so little moisture, and grow vigorously enough to be just as well adapted here as our native species.

It was the immigrants of the goldfields who first brought the black locust from the East and Midwest. The trees are thought to have originated in the Appalachian region. There they were of great value because the wood of the locust is very hard and resistant to decay. Before the availability of redwood, this was an essential material for any use where the earth or water contacts the wood, such as with a railroad tie. It stands to reason pioneers wishing to plant trees for fence posts and even mine timbers would be eager to plant their locust seed in the new land. With the advent of electricity, locust wood was preferred for pins which supported the old-fashioned glass insulators on utility poles.

Current efforts are underway in Boston Harbor to restore the historic U.S.S. *Constitution,* or "Old Ironsides," which was constructed in 1797, using a variety of woods, such as oak and pine. As a ship of war, no expense was spared in using the strongest, most durable materials available at that time. Beneath the iron plating, a beautiful wooden ship is revealed by high-tech x-ray photography. Black locust from Massachusetts plays an important but perhaps invisible structural role in this ship. It is used throughout as treenails, or trunnels, fasteners which hold the exterior planking to the futtocks, the ship's internal ribs. Shipbuilding throughout the nineteenth century continued to utilize locust for these crucial connections, which attests to its proven over time.

The black locust is often confused with its relative the honey locust (*Gleditsia triacanthos*). The species name, *pseudoacacia*, refers to the similarity of this tree to the acacia, which is also highly drought-tolerant, sometimes thorny, and equally brittle. Black locust foliage was valuable as horse fodder in Europe and served as a substitute for indigo as a blue dye. The yellow flowers, possibly of honey locust but also of black locust, were used by the Chinese for a yellow dye.

Locust trees tend to sucker heavily, and seedlings pop up all around the mother tree, which can become a nuisance in more restricted gardens. Like other drought-resistant species, they are invasively rooted, as dangerous to sewer and water lines as the willow. This rapid and extensive rooting has led to the black locust's being used for slope stabilization and erosion control. Old black locusts are not often well shaped, because their brittle wood tends to break apart in storms. This weak branching is a hazard to consider before selecting the locust as a landscape tree.

The locust has one great enemy, the locust borer, which decimated the trees in the Eastern states. The borer is not so common in California, and fortunately many of our historic trees still stand. The locust may soon face the same problem as the American elm if its parasites gain a foothold in the West.

Black locust is an important landscape tree in the desert communities, where other shade trees struggle in the dry heat. The beautiful cultivar 'Purple Robe' is by far the most beautiful of the true black locusts. Another species growing in popularity is the Idaho locust, *Robinia ambigua* 'Idahoensis', which is less invasive and stronger branching, with large, pink flower clusters.

Victorian Oddities—Only in California

Dragon's blood dracaena and tower-of-jewels best represent how exotic plants appealed to residents of balmy California during the botanical craze of the latter nineteenth century. They do not fill any particular niche and are not very attractive, either. It is the fact that they are tropical oddities that made them most desirable, for the homeowner wealthy enough to display this kind of rare plant material was surely the most socially respected. These plants can now be found only as remnants of Victorian gardens, attesting to their inability to prove themselves worthwhile over the long term. Yet when I see the tower-of-jewels in bloom, or pass close by the cylindrical branches of a very old dragon tree, I am reminded how diverse this universe of plants truly is, and I cannot help but grow thankful for those pioneering souls who first brought them here for us to share in their mystery.

Dragon's Blood Dracaena, Dragon Tree
Dracaena Draco

The Victorian quest for ever more exotic landscape plants was sure to eventually come around to planting the dragon's blood dracaena. A close relative of our dracaena houseplants, it originated in the Canary Islands off the west coast of Africa. It is very long-lived, with a seventy-foot specimen on Tenerife Island estimated to be close to 6,000 years old, although this age is debatable. At any rate, these succulent plants are members of the lily family and attain treelike proportions with age. Frost-tender, the only sizable California specimens today are found on the southern coastline; some fine examples are out in front of Sherman Gardens in Corona Del Mar, and others are at the Hotel Del Coronado in the San Diego area.

This plant has a unique place in the botanical world, for it was important in the occult arts as providing "dragon blood" substitute, although Venetian traders often sold it as the real thing. The fruit and sap of the female trees is bright red and dries into hard, blood-colored beads. The material was associated with love potions in medieval times. It was burned by deserted wives and maidens for an aphrodisiac incense, actually emitting benzoic acid. If burned by an open window in a lonely bedchamber at seven midnights in a row, the escaping fumes would bring back the straying husband or lover.

Tower-of-Jewels
Echium Wildpretii

I have seen this unusual plant grow and bloom only in the seacoast town of Mendocino, a Victorian jewel of a village with period architecture carefully restored and preserved. The pride of Madeira (*Echium fastuosum*) is a common shrubby perennial which grows up and down the California coastline, easily recognized by its candles of iridescent purple blooms. Tower-of-jewels is a close relative that has not been widely cultivated since the nineteenth century. The remnants of what must have been a popular exotic plant still readily reseed themselves in Mendocino, attesting to its ease of germination and preference for the mild climate there.

Echium wildpretii is a biennial, blooming in its second year. The seedlings develop into compact rosettes of foliage; when mature, they send out very tall, purple flower spires up to three feet long, sometimes even larger. The common name, tower-of-jewels, was derived from these glittering stalks of blooms. Once it flowers and goes to seed, the plant dies, but its persistence is ensured by seedlings eager to sprout. Echiums in general prefer well-drained, relatively infertile soil, so the coastal sand provides a perfect germinating medium. Like the dragon's blood dracaena, tower-of-jewels is a bizarre remnant of the heyday of botanical extravagance stimulated by the mild California climate.

KATE O. SESSIONS

Though Kate Sessions (1857–1940) was dead long before I was born, she lived on through her nephew, Milton P. Sessions. While studying horticulture in Santa Rosa, California, I took a job as part-time gardener for a large ranch up on the Russian River. Upon meeting my eighty-year-old employer, I was startled to find him a landscape architect and well versed in my chosen field. Over the first few months, he shared his story about how he learned his trade from his aunt, Kate Sessions. Milton resembled her and displayed the same boundless energy and compulsive drive, like none I have ever known since.

Under his tutelage I began to read about Kate and discovered she was well educated, was dedicated to horticulture, and remained single her entire life. She was born in the San Francisco Bay area during the height of the Victorian era and attended the University of California at Berkeley, graduating in 1881. Her final thesis was "The Natural Sciences as a Field for

Kate Sessions, 1932. (*San Diego Historical Society*)

Women's Labors," and, although she is not documented to have taken agriculture courses, it is thought she probably did take some, along with other sciences. This period did not see many women of higher learning, and the mere fact she did obtain a degree is noteworthy.

Kate began teaching in Oakland public schools but was offered a position in a newly formed school district in San Diego. She moved to the remote, small city in the south to begin teaching, but due to administrative difficulties took another position in San Gabriel. While she was away, friends bought the San Diego Nursery and in 1885 became partners with Kate, who had exhibited a keen interest in the developing commercial agriculture of southern California.

Kate's interest in floriculture began to take form, and she sent to San Francisco for plants that she knew were frost-tender to see whether they would grow outdoors in her new home. Before long she had attained a variety of exotics and was growing them in greater numbers to be sold at the San Diego Nursery or her florist shop downtown. This was fortuitous, for she was well established by the time of the land boom of 1886, when the new-comers demanded trees, for much of the town was nothing but sage-covered coastal bluffs. When Coronado Island was developed, Kate and her partners obtained lots there and moved the growing operation to the milder climate.

San Diego was developing rapidly into a coastal resort. A vast number of exotic plants were being grown on the island for the gardens of the new Hotel Del Coronado. Once the site was planted, Kate took over disposal of the leftover materials, which fueled her avid interest in exotics such as palms. She began writing for newspapers and periodicals to help promote the new plants for sale in her nursery. The hotel had forced land values in Coronado to skyrocket, and the growing grounds there had become too small for her expanded operation.

She managed to negotiate with the city of San Diego to lease a portion of fourteen hundred acres designated for a park. She was required to supply one hundred trees per year to improve the almost treeless site in exchange for using the land. This move was the first step in her being later named City Gardener and "the Mother of Balboa Park."

Kate thrived on the new site and supplied her flower shop from plants grown there along with trees and shrubs. She was fully involved in her business of growing and selling cut flowers and landscape plants. She clung to her long skirts but had special reinforced pockets added to contain her clippers and other important materials. Rarely was she seen without her sturdy boots and felt hat. Life centered around her plants.

During this time she was instrumental in propagating and popularizing many of the newly introduced species, most exotic and discovered in faraway places with climates similar to that of southern California. Her favorites were palms, and many of her regal plantings still line the older streets of town. She maintained a vast correspondence network with other nurserymen and horticulturists in order to keep abreast of new introductions and obtain them. Her successful business and horticultural accomplishments became well known throughout the West.

By the turn of the century, the park was under development, and the required trees, along with many more, had been planted. Kate moved her nursery to Mission Hills, where she continued her network of exchanging seed with such notables as Luther Burbank. She supplied trees and plants for Henry E. Huntington's estate in San Marino. By the 1920s, development again pushed her out, now to Pacific Beach. She had become the most well-respected ornamental floral and plant expert in southern California and grew more active socially with age.

In 1939 her lifetime achievement was honored by the award of the Frank N. Meyer Medal for distinguished service in flower and plant introduction. She was credited with importing and promoting the queen palm (*Arecastrum romanzoffianum*), bougainvillea, *Juniperus chinensis* 'Torulosa', and a wide assortment of iceplants and their kin. She was a primary source of many Australian species, such as eucalypts, acacias, and melaleuca. In 1940 Kate died at 82 while in hospital for a broken hip.

There is much to tell about this unique woman, who was such a part of the Victorian age yet evolved with time to flourish in the twentieth century. Milton Sessions took over some of her businesses enterprises and was Commissioner of Balboa Park for ten years. I became his protegee during my time in Santa Rosa, and to this day I credit Kate with beginning this wonderful legacy, which was ultimately bequeathed to me.

THE DETAILS: REDWOODS AND GOLD DUST

The Victorian gardens were the first in the West to display the ornamental elements of classical European landscapes. Just as the people collected plants, they also gathered up decorative items to highlight parts of their gardens. Those who were newly wealthy and wished to emulate the "good taste" of their European predecessors tended to overdo their decoration, just as they did inside the house. Even someone who was not wildly rich or successful believed that the accumulation of this kind of ornament would give the impression of greater social standing.

Frontyard Fences

It is important to realize that during this time people did not move quickly. They were still dependent on horse and buggy or traveled about on foot. While passing a house, there was time to admire the garden and appreciate every small detail. People who were successful often sought to separate themselves from their more humble beginnings, and many believed the elaborate fences around the frontyards were designed to divide the home of the upwardly mobile from the rabble of the street. The expense of the fence was also a more direct statement as to the owner's financial standing.

Cast or wrought iron fencing was the pinnacle of both cost and detail. These were long-lasting and very strong enclosures. Today a cast iron fence is prohibitive to even well-heeled homeowners; wrought iron is more affordable but sometimes fails to project the desired character. During the Victorian times the wood picket fences were designed to new heights of detailing. The fences often mirrored the same gingerbread patterns of the house and were almost always painted white.

The Gazebo or Summerhouse

The lot of women during this time was not easy. Heavy clothing, tight corsets, and a general lack of exercise made California's summer heat waves unbearable. The popularity of gazebos or summerhouses was created by the need for cooler outdoor spaces shaded from the hot sun. There women could spend the hours outdoors and be able to enjoy the garden in relative comfort.

The gazebo obtained its name because it allowed the user to "gaze about" the garden in all directions. Hexagons were easier to build than round structures, although some buildings were square. It was a romantic notion that the gazebo be shrouded in vines to make it a moody refuge and more natural in character. The gazebo could be made of any material from cast iron to wood, and some even had glass windows.

Today the enchantment of gazebos is returning, and they are growing more common as outdoor living spaces. A gazebo may be built from scratch by using modern plans available to homeowners, but due to the hexagonal shape, construction can be difficult. Packages of premilled, ready-to-assemble materials are growing in popularity, but these can be very expensive. A gazebo becomes more usable if there is electricity supplied for fans and heaters. Screen panels can transform it into a bug-free outdoor dining area.

Rock Walls

After the railroad was built and the mines played out, there was an enormous population of Chinese laborers living in California. Seen as a source of cheap labor, they were hired by ranchers and farmers to gather up stones from their fields. These stones were then stacked into dry stone walls, which are still standing today as mute testimony to the backbreaking work required to build them. Some fine examples can be found in the lower foothills of the Sutter Buttes and in the rolling grasslands south of Chico.

A rock wall does not erode or rot and is destined to remain in place indefinitely. There are many old homesites throughout the rockier portions of the state which were built upon these dry stone foundations, and miners in treeless portions of the foothills built their cabins entirely of stone. In Downieville there is some fine rock work using a unique type of flat slate found there, and the walls still stand today without steel or mortar as reinforcement.

Coleman residence in Grass Valley. Though a modest home by Victorian standards, there are still the twin urns by the front gate, where every passerby might appreciate them.

Ornaments

If you were to visit Blenheim Palace in England, Versailles in France, or practically any Italian villa, you'd find the same ornaments which popped up in Victorian gardens. This is primarily because the newly rich of America sought to reflect in their own "palaces" the opulence of European royalty. One of the most widely used ornaments was the urn, shaped much like a wineglass, which often flanked a front entry or marked the corners of a planter. There were no particular rules about urns except that they were desirable. I have seen photos of the most primitive farmhouses, where out in front are a pair of stone urns placed on either side of a dirt walkway. Urns were often planted with exotics such as yucca or New Zealand flax so they would be noticed in the prominent containers.

Victorian gardens also utilized statuary. A sundial became a central focus for carpet bedding or as a hub for the walkways which often snaked through the plantings. Seating was also carefully placed to provide a rest to corseted women, who could not breathe well under the exertion of strolling the garden.

6

PRESERVING AND
REVIVING THE
PAST

*a*s California's population increases, the need for expanded housing cannot be ignored. Residential areas and entire new towns are moving into previously undeveloped lands. In many cases, this land may hold long-abandoned historic sites, described in environmental impact reports as cultural resources. Sites identified by archaeologists are dealt with in a number of ways, depending on their significance. Some are ultimately abandoned, others fully restored, and still more documented and protected.

Often sites of eighteenth- and nineteenth-century human habitation may be marked by only a few tenacious plants bearing no resemblance to the surrounding vegetation. The nature of these plants has a tremendous bearing on the future treatment of the place. For example, there may be no remnant of an adobe house melted away by the rain long ago. But a prickly pear hedge or even a single palm, such as that used for execution by firing squad in San Diego, does attest to once-thriving settlements. Prickly pear is easily propagated from cuttings, but to transplant such an immense spiny plant is unreasonable. In this case, propagation is the most feasible way to move and preserve the old hedge. Just as a pottery shard unearthed at a dig is moved and preserved at a museum for display, plants can be either transplanted to a new, protected site or propagated to protect its offspring.

In the case of a native oak, which can be neither transplanted nor vegetatively propagated, preservation becomes more complex. A native oak, particularly a very old one, not only defies transplanting, it is very touchy about soil disturbance in and around its dripline. Should this type of historic plant be located in the path of development, the general approach is to establish it as a historic site and legally protect it by various techniques.

Both these examples show why preservation of historic plants becomes complicated. It is an issue influenced by many factors—plant site, climate, government input, species, among others. In the cases of such civic organizations as tree foundations or historical societies, private resources may be all that is available for preservation. Our state's economic situation is precarious, and the likelihood of financial assistance by public agencies for historic plant preservation is dwindling. That is why it is important that citizens of the state become more aware of historical plants and their intrinsic value to future generations.

WHAT ARE HEIRLOOM SPECIES?

An heirloom species is one close to the original strains first brought into cultivation from the wild. They are often very different from our modern strains, but contain an enormous gene pool of traits that assist in adaptation to changing environments. Not every gene in the pool will be exhibited at the same time in an individual plant. For example, the gene pool for a sunflower may contain a hundred traits, but only about fifty of them may be displayed in a given wild sunflower plant. The other fifty may be recessive or otherwise appear only once in a while.

Controlled breeding of plants crosspollinates numerous individuals to produce generation after generation of seedlings in the hope that the sheer number of offspring will result in the appearance of one of the recessive genes. A good example is the 'Swan Hills' olive tree, which is valuable for landscaping because it produces no flowers or fruit. A farmer grew an entire orchard of olive trees from seeds, and one of these seeds contained the recessive gene that rendered the resulting tree sterile. Once orchards the trees grew old enough to flower, the sterile tree was discovered. The chances of a fruitless tree occurring again by seed are slim, so cuttings were taken to produce many new trees with exactly the same genetic recipe. This illustrates how variable seedlings can be and why vegetative propagation is important when preserving very old, historic plants which cannot be moved.

If a recessive gene is harvested from the gene pool, another gene or trait must be exchanged. Sometimes the exchange for a new flower color means the plant relinquishes its disease resistance or robust growth habits. Sometimes the exchange is less obvious but nevertheless occurs. Therefore, selective breeding of plants can leave the species less durable in the long run as we encourage the recessive genes to appear and exchange others which may or may not be of immediate value.

A good example is the potato, which originated in the Andes Mountains of Peru and was long cultivated by the Incas. Their potato is small and purple, but centuries of selective breeding brought out characteristics of white flesh, large tubers, and more prolific crops, yielding the potatoes we eat today. But that old Peruvian potato produces far better in low-fertility soils and may actually be distasteful to many potato pests. It could even have considerably greater resistance to frost damage. Hence, the trade-off for better size and flavor resulted in plants more finicky about their growing conditions.

There is a strong movement today to preserve original varieties of food plants in seed banks because many are no longer commercially cultivated. Botanists and plant scientists are concerned that if they become extinct, the entire gene pool they contain is also lost. In the future, as agricultural methods and the environment changes, some of these genes may be helpful to developing new and better adapted plants. But if the species is lost, we lose these options as well.

One of the finest examples of Western heirloom variety preservation is Native Seeds/SEARCH, a nonprofit conservation, research, and education organization. This group has actively sought out the seeds planted by southwestern Native Americans in the United States and northern Mexico. These strains, under cultivation by these peoples for centuries, are well adapted to the dry climate and high temperatures of desert ecosystems. Someday in the future, if we were to experience a climate change and diminishing rainfall, these tough varieties of the past may be the salvation of American agriculture.

Although plants included in this book are not necessarily agricultural, their gene pools may someday become important. If we cannot save original plants, their seed or new plants grown from cuttings will ensure the gene pool remains intact for posterity. Many plant preservationists and botanists are avid in supporting heirloom-species genetics for this reason. Others are more concerned about preserving the actual original plants, as are members of heirloom oak tree societies.

Plants as Historic Monuments

Throughout California, archaeologists and botanists can find historic sites simply by vegetation. Every plant that is not native, and some that are, were brought here by either man or animal. The lone palm often marks the refuse site for a homestead, or sometimes it is the last remnant of a long-forgotten dooryard garden. A lichen-encrusted apple tree in our foothill regions generally indicates the presence of a farm or house close by. This can also apply to native plants as well, although these sites are not quite as obvious. Some black oak groves have cropped up around the bedrock mortars of California Native American villages. Those plants that are most drought-tolerant and hardy enough to grow on nothing more than natural rainfall are the true landmarks of our state, and if they could, they would speak volumes about the people in their past.

PRESERVATION MOVEMENTS

There is a growing interest throughout America to bring these historic plants to people everywhere. One of the most active is a program of the American Forestry Association in Washington, D.C. It began in 1978 when Henry Clepper, a historian for A.F.A. began cataloging the very largest known examples of each species of tree. These were compiled into the annual *Famous and Historic Trees of America*. People across the country were encouraged to measure and submit their largest specimens so that the nation's greatest trees could be duly recognized. The list is constantly being revised and updated.

One offspring enterprise of this listing is a documentation of very old trees at historic sites. This directly links an individual plant to an event or time, making it a living remnant of our nation's growth. Such a tree may not be the largest example of its species, but its role in history is verified. For example, a two-hundred-foot-tall ponderosa pine in the Sierra gold country was long ago marked with a blaze to show the main trail running the length of the Mother Lode (now California Highway 49). New seedlings grown from its cones can be purchased through the Famous and Historic Trees Project catalog.

Anyone interested in helping preserve plants from historic sites may join any one of the growing number of organizations dedicated to such work. In some cases, the best way to know which plants are indeed historic is to become familiar or active in local historical societies. Often these people have vast knowledge of long-forgotten sites where important plants may still be living.

One of the biggest problems encountered by these groups is finding a place capable of accepting and nurturing relocated historic plants. As discussed earlier, government funding is dwindling, and many city, county, and state botanical gardens and arboretums are experiencing dire financial straits. Those on college and university campuses rely heavily on students for much of the work. Even privately owned gardens open to the public are suffering, with volunteers doing more and more of the work. In most cases, a loyal crew of volunteers is all that keeps their doors open, for it requires a tremendous amount of labor to maintain a healthy and attractive garden of any size. This is the primary reason why historic plants often succumb to developers: There is no funding to move or propagate them, and even then, new sites are scarce.

Salvage and Rescue

Anyone interested in historic plants can act on his or her own to salvage plants from condemned sites. Seedlings, cuttings, and even some transplants can make your backyard into a storehouse of history. It is essential that you not gather plants from public sites without authorization. Plants on private land also require permission from the owner prior to access and salvage. Plants in the wild are also off-limits for the most part, but there are exceptions. For example, if an oak tree is scheduled to be removed, and this is verified with the owner or proper authority, it is fine to collect acorns. In fact, this is the best source for reestablishing groves destined for the bulldozer, because a large sampling of seeds will contain nearly the entire gene pool of its wild predecessors.

Good candidates for salvage include plants that readily sprout from seed or strike roots on a cutting. Obtain a basic plant propagation book to find out which are the easiest to propagate.

SOME EASILY PROPAGATED PLANTS OF
THE OLD WEST

Oak Trees
Grow from Seed

Collect acorns in the fall, store them for a month in the refrigerator, then germinate in sand or perlite. Once an acorn is cracked and the tip of root begins to show, plant it on its side three to six inches deep in the location it is to grow. Collect more acorns than you need, allowing for natural mortality.

California Fan Palm
Transplant or Grow from Seed

Palms transplant easily with a small rootball because, like cacti, they keep their moisture in water-holding vessels within the trunk. Young seedlings may be transplanted by hand; larger plants are very heavy and should be moved by a professional tree company. In many urban areas, seedlings can be found growing beneath a fertile palm, and these can be easily dug up and moved.

The easiest method of propagating a palm is by planting seed, which will readily sprout if there is sufficient moisture. Palms sprout and grow well in pots if given adequate drainage and a light soil mix.

Agave americana
Cuttings

The big blue, spiked agave naturally develops multiple pups attached to the base of the mother plant by long roots. These pups can be easily severed and should be taken with as much root attached as possible. If cut too close to its growing center, the pup may not be able to recover. Let the cutting air-dry for a few hours, until the wound has developed a dry callus. This helps discourage rotting. Plant the pup in sand or another light rooting medium, and keep moist until roots develop. Then plant out into garden soil.

Old Roses
Cuttings or Grow from Seed

Roses are very easy plants to propagate. The older varieties tend to be more vigorous and do not require grafting. There are two simple ways to propagate roses: from deciduous hardwood cuttings or from seed. Some people like to root soft green cuttings during the summer, but these are a bit more difficult. Cuttings ensure you will have a new plant identical to the parent; growing from seed is much more variable, depending on the varieties of the parents.

Deciduous hardwood cuttings are taken from dormant canes during the winter and are about six inches long. These can be cut while winter-pruning. Choose blemish-free wood that appears young and vigorous. Dip the bottom end into rooting hormone, set it into perlite or coarse sand, and keep it moist for a month or two. The cutting should strike a root within that time, but it will do so faster if provided with bottom heat. The end should develop a callus, from which roots will emerge. Exposure to warm air during this time may cause the cutting to send out a stem and leaves prematurely.

The rose hip is a seedpod that develops after flowers fade. It should remain on the plant to mature and turn red or orange when ripe. Extract the seeds and place them in a rooting tray or six-pack. Keep moist and warm. Keep in mind that growing from seed does not guarantee the same variety of rose as the mother plant. There will be diversity of both flower color and growth habit.

Prickly Pear Cactus
Cuttings

Most cacti and succulents are easy to propagate from cuttings. With prickly pear and chollas, it is essential you wear gloves and use barbecue tongs to handle the plants. Both of these cacti can be rooted from a single paddle or cigar-shaped leaf. They should be allowed to air-dry briefly to callus. The leaf can be planted a few inches deep into garden soil if it is well drained, or it will root easily in a sand-filled container. Keep moist but not wet.

Willow and Cottonwood
Cuttings

Trees that are water hunters have a remarkable ability to root from cuttings. In fact, these plants have fibrous root systems that do not develop properly in pots. In the ground a cutting will root so fast, there is no need to get it started in a container. The key is plenty of moisture. Some people take very large cuttings from these trees called poles. A pole can be dropped into a hole dug by a posthole digger, with a few feet sticking out at the top. This is a good method where there is threat of flooding along drainages, creeks, and rivers. An entire bank can be planted in willow by cutting branches in two-foot-long segments and inserting them into the soil. With sufficient moisture they will take root and help to stabilize the soil in that bank.

Take cuttings in early winter after leaves have fallen. Be sure to note which end is up, because sometimes it's hard to tell. The length of the cutting will vary, depending on the diameter of the wood. The most vigorous wood will be that which grew the summer before. If you lay the cutting down upon the soil and anchor it with coat hanger pins, it will root all along its length in a hedge of trees. This is helpful for erosion control on slopes, as privacy screens, or as windbreaks. As plants become established, they will grow much faster with plenty of water. Be cautious to avoid water, septic, and sewer lines when planting these water-loving trees.

Scotch Broom
Grow from Seed

The plants naturalized in the Sierra foothills have reproduced successfully from seed. Their consistent flower color illustrates there is not much diversity in seedlings. They require no special treatment for the seed to germinate. The seed may be collected in summer. Strip off the pod and soak in warm water for twenty-four hours, then plant an inch deep or so in sand or commercial seed-starter mix. Keep evenly moist.

Tree-of-Heaven
Cuttings

The male plants of this tree have an undesirable smell, so propagation should strive for only female plants. Since there is no control over sex with seedlings, only cuttings guarantee female plants. Tree-of-heaven grows readily from pieces of root. Select a female tree and dig around for some roots about the diameter of a knitting needle. Cut these into three-inch-long segments, plant them in a box of sand until they sprout, then transplant. Disturbed ground around a female tree might yield root suckers. Mother Nature has already done your propagation, so all you need to do is dig up the root during the winter, sever off the portion with the new growth, and transplant.

Black Locust
Grow from Seed

These trees have naturalized because of their readiness to germinate from seed, which has resulted in many thick, wild groves. Newer cultivars may not resemble their mothers when propagated from seed, but reproducing the more common older trees is simple. Collect seed in the fall and plant immediately where they are to grow in garden soil. The seed can be saved over winter and planted in spring, but this seems to reduce its vigor to sprout. You can also take suckers or root cuttings if available.

Blackberries
Layering

Wild blackberries are a good source of free plants for gardens, but beware of their invasive nature. These berries and other types of vine plants can be propagated by layering. To layer, select a long runner and bend it down so there is contact with the soil. First you can gently scar the underside of the runner with a knife, then apply rooting hormone. Stake the wounded portion to the ground with a wire coat hanger "bobby pin" and cover it with soil. The wound will root over the winter, and in spring the new plant may be severed from the old. For more detailed information on layering, consult a book on plant propagation.

APPENDIX

SOURCES FOR HEIRLOOM PLANTS AND SEEDS

Antique Rose Emporium
Route 5 Box 143
Brenham, TX 77833
Catalog $5.00.
Hundreds of heirloom rose varieties for warm-weather climates.

Heritage Rose Gardens
16831 Mitchell Creek Drive
Fort Bragg, CA 95437
Catalog $1.50.
Antique rose source for California.

Monticello, The Thomas Jefferson Center for Historic Plants
P.O. Box 316
Charlottesville, VA 22902
Free newsletter.
Nonprofit organization offering historic flowers, vines, and
vegetables.

Native Seeds/SEARCH
    2509 North Campbell Avenue #325
    Tucson, AZ 85719
    Catalog $1.00.
Southwestern Endangered Arid Land Resource Clearing House: a nonprofit conservation research and education organization. Source of seed cultivated by Native Americans in southwestern United States and Mexico.

    Plants of the Southwest
    1812 Second Street
    Santa Fe, NM 87501
    Catalog $1.00
Good mail-order source of southwestern plants.

    Roses of Yesterday and Today
    802 Brown's Valley Road
    Watsonville, CA 95076
    Catalog $2.00.
Mail-order source for many heirloom roses.

    Seeds Blum
    Idaho City Stage
    Boise, ID 83706
    Catalog $3.00
Heirloom cottage garden plants and vegetables.

    Seed Savers Exchange
    3076 North Winn Road
    Decorah, IA 52101
    (318) 382-5990
Annual membership $25.00. Brochure $1.00.
A nonprofit organization devoted to preserving heirloom seed for food crops. Acts as communication network linking members who buy and sell seed to one another. There's also The Flower and Herb Exchange at the same address.

    Seeds West
    P.O. Box 1739
    El Prado, NM 87529
    (505) 758-7268
    Catalog $2.00.
Heirloom seed for western climates.

BIBLIOGRAPHY

Austin, Mary. *The Land of Little Rain.* New York: Penguin, 1988.

Balls, Edward K. *Early Uses of California Plants.* Berkeley: University of California Press, 1962.

Barrott, S.A. and E.W. Gifford. *Miwok Material Culture: Indian Life of the Yosemite Region.* Yosemite: Yosemite Association, 1908.

Barrows, David Prescott. *Ethnobotany of the Cahuilla Indians.* Banning: Malki Museum Press, 1967. Reprint of a work published originally in 1900.

Bean, Lowell John, and Katherine Siwa Saubel. *Temalpakh: Cahuilla Indian Knowledge and Usage of Plants.* Banning: Malki Museum Press, 1972.

Blackburn, Thomas C., and Kat Anderson, editors. *Before the Wilderness: Environmental Management by Native Californians.* Menlo Park: Ballena Press, 1993.

Brewer, William H. *Up and Down California: In 1860–1864.* Berkeley: University of California Press, 1974.

Chestnut, V.K. *Plants Used by the Indians of Mendocino County, California.* Willits: Mendocino County Historical Society, 1974. This is a reprint of a work published in 1902. Reach the Mendocino County Historical Society at 603 West Perkins Street, Ukiah, CA 95482.

Coolidge, Dane. *California Cowboys.* Tucson: University of Arizona Press, 1967. A reprint of a 1939 book.

Dreyer, Peter. *A Gardener Touched with Genius: The Life of Luther Burbank.* Santa Rosa: Luther Burbank Home and Gardens. Available from Luther Burbank Home and Gardens, P.O. Box 1678, Santa Rosa, CA 95402.

Kroeber, A.L. *Handbook of the Indians of California.* New York: Dover Publications, Inc., 1976. Reprint of a 1925 book.

Lewis, Donovan. *Pioneers of California: True Stories of Early Settlers in the Golden State.* San Francisco: Scottwall Associates, 1993.

MacPhail, Elizabeth C. *Kate Sessions: Pioneer Horticulturist.* San Diego: The San Diego Historical Society, 1976. Available from the San Diego Historical Society, P.O. Box 81825, San Diego, CA 92138.

Ortiz, Beverly. *It Will Live Forever: Traditional Yosemite Indian Acorn Preparation.* Berkeley: Heyday Books, 1991.

Peattie, Donald Culross. *A Natural History of Western Trees.* Boston: Houghton Mifflin, 1953.

INDEX